# DELIVERED FROM EVIL

TULSA

# DELIVERED FROM EVIL

## FROM

# EVIL

## FROM FAME, ADDICTION, TO HOPE

## BY ANTHONY GREVE

ISBN: 978-1-954095-03-8
*Delivered from Evil*

Versions of the Holy Bible cited: ESV English Standard Version; NASB New American Standard Bible; NIV New International Version; NKJV New King James Version; NLT New Living Translation; TPT The Passion Translation

Editor: Rosalie LoPinto
Front and back cover photo credit: Steve Ziegelmeyer Photography
Page 82 and 83 photo credit: Aaron Steele

For permission requests, write to the publisher at the address below.

Yorkshire Publishing
1425 E 41st Pl
Tulsa, OK 74105
www.YorkshirePublishing.com
918.394.2665

Published in the USA

*This book is dedicated to my mother (Saniye), father (Larry), and brothers (Nolan and Greg), as well as the entire Greve and Bernay family. I love you, and God loves you.*

# CONTENTS

# INTRO

We had just pulled up in front of our hotel in Huntsville, Alabama, and our manager went to check us in. I was tired, extremely exhausted, from the road. The party lifestyle I had been indulging in for years certainly had imposed its share of wear and tear, and it was beginning to take a toll on me. I was rundown and wanted to rest, but I knew that we had to go out this evening. It's just something the band did. We would find a bar, usually be given VIP status, and once in, we would mingle with fans. We were on tour with Three Doors Down at the time, and we were indeed making a reputation for ourselves. But this night was different. I just didn't want to go out. I asked my tour manager at the time if I could have the night off. I didn't much feel like partying. His response was, "Absolutely." "As a matter of fact," he added, "here's the key to the hotel room, and it's all yours for the night. Me and the guys will be staying on the bus. Just make sure to meet us back down here at 10:00 am for bus call."

I grabbed a backpack and threw some clothes in it, excited to have a room to myself for the night and finally get some rest. This rest was much needed after the prolonged chaos of life on the road.

I made my way up to the hotel's second floor, entered the room, and set my bag down. After a few moments of sitting on the bed, I decided that I was going to take a bath ... but before continuing this story, I need to go back to the beginning.

# THE EARLY YEARS

As early as I can remember, I had so many dreams and aspirations. If there was one thing that God gave me, it was the ability to dream. Dreaming is what kept me going. So many people lose hope along the way, but it's important never to lose the capacity to dream.

My life was amazing growing up. I had a very full and better than average childhood. I'm the son of a Turkish mother and an American father. How did they meet, you ask? My dad was United States Military (Air Force) and based in Ankara, Turkey when he met my mother. They married overseas and later moved back to the States together. I came along in 1984. Four years later, my brother was born.

The first few years of my life were spent living in a little lakefront cottage. We had a dog named Ugly (in Turkish). My mother named him. On many occasions, a cousin of mine would strap me to his back, and we would go fishing. We were completely surrounded by nature. Though my memories from this time are few, I would spend a lot of time in my later years hanging out in this neck of the woods. Because so much of my family lived there, it would later get dubbed "Greve Land" by a friend of mine and me. There were plenty of areas to camp and lots of animals to see. Growing up, I would spend many days and nights out in Greve Land camping, fishing, dirt biking, and partying. I would also spend a lot of time overseas. My mother would take me to her homeland frequently, so I got to know both sides of my family, the American and the Turkish. I was also fluent in both English and Turkish from my earliest years. It was quite the gift to grow up bi-lingual and multi-cultural. I certainly had a grip on the American way of life, but my heart was filled with the Middle East. There was something about Turkey that always felt like home.

Growing up in the States, my parents would never let my brother or me drink soda as young kids, but when we were in Turkey, it was like being on vacation, so my mom would cut us a break. It also didn't hurt that Grandma was on our side. In general, it seemed like we could get away with way more over there. The first time I ever drank Coca-Cola was in Turkey. Because we were not allowed to have it back home, I didn't even know that it existed in the U.S. I came back sharing with everyone how Turkey had this amazing soft drink called Coca-Cola. Maybe it was time to free us from our sequestered environment a little bit. But Coca-Cola aside, I had a fantastic family and the best grandparents in the world.

I was always drawn to music, even as a small child. It so happened that there was a music store across the hall from my grandparents' condominium in Turkey. Sometimes, when our door was left open as Grandma was cleaning, I would sneak across the hall when she wasn't looking to check it out. Eventually, my mom would come looking for me and find me mulling around the music store. "What are you doing?!" she'd ask in a slightly agitated voice. The owner would say, "It's okay! The kid's an artist. He is going to be a musician." So, as I reflect on it now, I can see that this was declared and spoken over me at a young age.

The music store owner would let me mess around on the instruments even though I was very little and didn't know what I was doing. And, though I didn't own a real guitar at the time, I did have a toy Pink Panther guitar; when I was home, I would hammer away on it like it was the real thing. What I didn't realize was that I was already getting direction for my future. Music always seemed to be a part of my life though it wouldn't be until years later that I would pursue it as a career.

I must have been between three and four years old when we moved from the cottage into our first home. It wasn't long after that my prayer request was answered for a baby brother. Nolan Nathaniel Greve was named after pro baseball player Nolan Ryan. I loved my little brother. My mom would place him on the front of my four-wheeler Power Wheels, and we'd cruise around the yard. Our cruising didn't last long since he would always try to take control of the vehicle. One memory I will never forget is my mom going to take a shower and leaving me to watch him. When she finished showering, she was thrown into a panic because she couldn't find us in the house. I had taken Nolan outside, where we were playing in a puddle that had accumulated in front of the house. That might as well have been a lake to us! We were in the middle of a full-blown thunderstorm, and it was pouring as we blissfully splashed away in the puddle. Sadly, somewhere along the way, this kind of innocence is lost.

This era of my life was filled with Ghost Busters, Teenage Mutant Ninja Turtles, New Kids on the Block, and eventually Kris Kross—it should be very evident that I grew up in the mid to late

'80s and early '90s. *Nightmare on Elm Street* was a hit movie, and it wasn't long before I would develop an interest in horror films.

Once we were a bit older, my mom would send my brother and me to spend our summers with Grandma and Grandpa in Turkey. Upon our arrival, one of the first things my grandparents would do was take us to the local amusement park. We loved going and had a blast every time. At this park, you had to pay an entrance fee in addition to paying for each individual ride, but Grandma and Grandpa didn't mind. They would let us go on as many rides as we wanted to. We would then travel a good eight hours by car to their summer house. This was where we would spend the majority of our time during these summer vacations. It was sort of a resort-style condominium community. Everyone knew each other. It was like the *Cheers* theme song, "where everybody knows your name." The vacationers at this resort who came year after year became very close-knit. We had the time of our lives there. We would spend our days on the beach along the Marmara Sea having jellyfish wars, swimming, and kayaking. For young boys, this life was amazing!

# A STEP INTO THE INDUSTRY

I was about six years old when my parents got divorced. No one gets married planning to divorce, but it happens. My brother was too young to understand what was going on truly. I remember climbing into my mom's lap to comfort her on one of those difficult nights during the divorce process. She sat on the couch in the living room crying and saying, "What am I going to do?" I kept telling her, "It's going to be okay, Mom." It was a difficult time for all of us. My mom found another house in town that she moved into taking my brother and me with her. Though my parents were separated, we saw our dad anytime we wanted to. They always got along and made it work for the sake of my brother and me. Nolan and I would go back and forth between the two houses at will.

As a kid, I got into martial arts courtesy of both the Ninja Turtles and my parents. I was a huge Turtles fan and wanted to be one for the rest of my life. I was a very serious kid, and I took my karate seriously. This was my first real passion in life. I studied a Japanese form of Karate called *Okinawa Te*. I fell in love with Jean

Claude Van Damme's movies. *Bloodsport* became one of my favorite movies. I also studied books by the late Bruce Lee. I spent years studying the art and worked my way up to a brown belt, which in that sect of karate was right below the highest level, the black belt.

One time, in the schoolyard in third grade, I got it in my head to pick a fight with the class bully. I remember having seen Van Damme in a movie and his opponent, and he took turns kicking each other in the ribs while Thai boxing, so I challenged the kid to the same type of fight. I wanted to be like my hero. This did not work out in my favor. He was much bigger than I was, and after a couple of kicks to the ribs, I was done.

Since I was into martial arts, my parents would take me to martial arts competitions where I would enroll to compete and see some of the best fighters in the world. There were some amazing competitors in those tournaments. I was completely amazed at some of the men and women I watched spar and perform *katas*. Karate had truly become my life.

From a young age, I was destined to be a performer. I loved being in front of people and performing for them. One day I came home from school and told my dad that he had to take me to the evening tryouts for a local talent show. I had found out about it in a newspaper clipping. I wanted to make the most of my gift as well as share it with others. While others would play instruments or sing a song in the talent show, I was going to perform a martial arts *kata* that I had put together to none other than the song, "Eye of the Tiger." This was going to be epic. I made the cut. This was my first performance in front of a real audience. I didn't place that day, but I did get some experience under my belt. I met a gentleman there who would soon become an integral part of my life. He was a classical guitarist as well as a guitar instructor and was in the talent show as well. About a year later, I would be reconnecting with him for lessons.

At school, I was making new friends and connecting with a different crowd. More and more, I started getting into music, and my passion and love for it was growing every day. It seemed that what was spoken over me at the music store across the hall from my grandmother's place was beginning to blossom. Romantic by nature, I was a huge R & B fan. I loved groups like All for One and Boyz II Men. One weekend, my friend Malcolm came to stay over and brought his dad's tape collection with him. I had no interest in rock and roll at that time. He had to convince me to give it a shot. It was at this time that I was introduced to bands such as Aerosmith, AC/DC, and Jackyl. I would end up doing shows with Jackyl down the road. Although I was starting to get into the rock scene, I couldn't give up my R & B quite yet. As I said, I was a romantic.

By this time, my dad had remarried. I was about ten years old. My stepbrother and I were dating twins. We had this idea of having them over for a candlelit dinner. I had my mom pick up sparkling grape juice for the occasion simply because it looked like wine. My brother's date ended up not coming, so it was just my girl, Rhonda, and me. I set the place up like a pro. I had soft music playing in the background, sparkling grape juice in wine glasses, and we ate a delicious meal of Beef Ramen noodles that my eldest stepbrother had made. One summer, I brought a bracelet back from Turkey for Rhonda. It was crystal all the way around. One night, I even went so far as to sing, "I Swear," by All for One to her over the phone. These were romantic yet innocent times in my life. The innocence was only temporary.

As my love for music increased, martial arts took a back seat. "I Swear," which I had sung to Rhonda, became one of my favorite songs. While in Turkey, I would practice singing it over and over again on our balcony. I would pretend that I was one of the members of the group performing. Then, one day, something happened that I hadn't anticipated; I was forced to sing in public.

At my grandparents' summer place, a restaurant served as a public meeting place for the people of the community. People from our community would meet there for dinner, to talk, or play a game of backgammon or cards. OK was a popular game at that time as well. On one of those summer nights, they had brought in entertainment, a keyboardist who would play and sing an array of the best Turkish songs. I was running around playing hide-and-go-seek in the garden with friends.

Typically, we would get yelled at for playing on the manicured grass. But on this occasion, I remember my grandfather coming up to me and saying, "I talked to the entertainer, and he is going to let you get up there and sing a song." I told my grandfather that I couldn't do that. He told me that he had already made the arrangements and that if I didn't, he would never speak to me again. He then proceeded to walk away. At that point, the pressure was on. I'm sure he would have spoken to me again, and that probably wasn't the best way to motivate me. On top of my grandfather's pressure, all of my friends joined in pressuring me to do it. I finally agreed. I got up there on the stage. It was quiet. It was as if the whole city was out that night, and that moment had all been set up just for me. I took a breath, and then I sang. The people loved it, and I received a standing ovation.

Now that we knew I could perform, my cousin and I came up with an idea to have a community talent show. This would be an opportunity for all of the local kids to show off their gifts. We cut out tickets that we handwrote on pieces of paper and sold them to the community people. My grandmother made us keep the price extra low. I would again sing, "I Swear." The kid who hosted the event even dressed in a tux. It was classic. It was amazing to see all the parents and grandparents out there supporting us. What a fantastic night it was. This was my first real step into show business, and I loved it indeed.

# PARADISE CITY AND A SIX STRING

I was watching MTV at my grandparents' house in Turkey when I saw a band that would change my life forever. The song in their music video would give me a new direction. If I wasn't sold out on rock music before, I was now. I was enamored. Years later, I would get this band's guitarist tattooed on the back of my forearm. I instantly fell in love with this guitarist and singer duo. The two of them were none other than Slash and Axle Rose. The band was Guns N' Roses, and the song was "Paradise City." I couldn't get it out of my head, nor could I stop singing it. I would walk around the house all day singing as much of it as I could remember. The song had a great hook, and they got me with it.

One day my grandmother said to me, "We are going down to the cassette store and getting you that tape." Though virtually obsolete today, a cassette was the medium for listening to music at that time. It was the successor to vinyl and the precursor to CDs. I was so excited. The following day my grandma took me to the cassette store, which was not even a mile from the house. We walked together arm in arm. I was around ten years old. When we got to the store, my grandmother asked me to tell the man what tape I wanted so that she could purchase it for me. The only problem was, I didn't know the name of the band, and I couldn't remember the name of the song. She kept telling me to sing it for him. Reluctantly, I finally did. He knew exactly what song I was singing. He reached over and pulled "Appetite for Destruction" off the shelf. My life would never be the same again. I could not wait to get home and listen to it.

From the moment I put it in the cassette player, I was hooked. I was a GNR (Guns N' Roses) fan for life. As far as I was concerned, this was the best thing I'd ever heard. Guns N' Roses was the band that turned the tide for me and truly got me into rock and roll. The guitar riff to "Nightrain" stole my heart. I would listen to the album every day. It stayed in my tape player for a while. I would crank it up as loud as I could and jump up on the couch like it was a stage, playing air guitar and singing along to it. At times I would use a tennis racket as my guitar.

One day while I was rocking out on the couch, I looked over and saw some of the neighborhood kids watching me through the window. I was so embarrassed that I jumped down and hid. Guns N' Roses would open the door to other bands that I would get into such as Aerosmith, Metallica, and eventually Pantera.

I noticed that my desires were shifting. Karate didn't mean as much to me anymore. All I wanted to do was listen to rock music. This led to me getting my first guitar. Since I wasn't interested in martial arts anymore, and I didn't want to play sports, my mother demanded that I do something. She suggested that I pick up an instrument. She took me down to a music store called Rick's Musik. The owners there absolutely loved me. When my mother suggested a band instrument, I said, "No way!" I was going to be like Slash. When I told her that I wanted to play guitar she said, "Honey, I don't think they have one in your size." One of the employees checked to see if they had something that was suitable for me, and sure enough, they did. They had one little acoustic hidden in the back just for me. There wasn't even a case for it, so we brought it home in the box. It was a tiny little child-sized acoustic that was dark brown with a deep reddish tint.

I couldn't put that guitar down; when I would go to sleep, I would put it in the bed next to me. I would write and make up songs on it before I even knew what I was doing. My parents soon realized that I was serious about this and decided to get me some lessons. I took one guitar lesson at Rick's. The instructor was a true rocker named Ted. That would be not only my first but my last lesson at Rick's for a while. My parents weren't able to keep taking me there at the time because of the distance. They also thought that maybe I should start with something a little more conventional.

My parents remembered the classical guitar player from the talent show that I had been in and set me up with him. I learned chords and how to read sheet music. He taught me the basics. I learned songs such as "Ode to Joy" and "Michael Row the Boat Ashore" in their simplest forms. But I was very serious and a perfectionist. When I did something, I did it with all my heart. There were times when I would make my whole family sit in the living room and listen to me play. I would attempt to play a song straight through, but I'd get frustrated and just start all over when I'd mess up. I wouldn't let anyone leave the room until I made it through the song. This became about a half-hour long event. Minus my mistakes, it should have taken three minutes. Needless to say, I was determined.

After about a year with the classical instructor, there wasn't much more he could do for me considering the direction I wanted to follow. I wanted to rock. He recommended a rock guitar instructor who was taking lessons from him at the time to get some classical playing under his belt. Believe it or not, he sent me to Ted – the guy I had taken my very first lesson from. Later on, during my Pop Evil days, Ted would come out on the road and do some tech work for the guys and me. He played a very significant role in my life. He was like a father to me.

Once I got a little older, Ted would take me into the bars with him, where I would sit and watch him play. I loved watching him play. He was so good, the best. I would just sit there and watch him all night. I wanted to learn as much as I could from him. By the time I was in my early teens and had gotten a little better, Ted would let me get up and play some songs with the band. One of those songs was "Where the River Flows," by Collective Soul. I rocked that thing. This was an exciting time in my life. Around this time, I would dye my hair funky colors, get my first real girlfriend, and begin broadening my musical horizons by getting into bands such as Green Day (which inspired the hair dye). I could never seem to get my hair as bright and vibrant as Green Day's vocalist, Billie Joe, got his. My first attempt at dyeing my hair was with Kool-Aid. Someone had recommended it. It didn't work; all it did was turn my scalp green. It would have probably worked better had I bleached my hair first, but nobody had mentioned that beforehand.

Green Day's album "Dookie" had just come out, and I was a huge fan. They had great songs, a great sound, and awesome hooks. More than the skill, I loved the aura and attitude that they carried. They were punk. I hadn't been introduced to punk before.

It was at this time that I got my first electric guitar. Like my acoustic, it was a knockoff brand, but it was great. It played like a champ. I wouldn't get into learning Guns N' Roses songs until later. They were still a bit complicated for where I was at musically. But Ted would teach me Green Day songs, and that's when I first learned how to play power chords. Those chords had the real rock sound that I was looking. Before I knew power chords, I would just play open chords on my acoustic. Once I grabbed hold of power chords, it was on! It was powerful, indeed. I would later get into punk bands like Rancid. They had an album out called, *And Out Come the Wolves*. It was my favorite album for a long time. These guys were a punk band that was completely punk yet palatable enough to be mainstream. They also had a bit of a reggae feel to them. The first time I saw them on MTV, I realized that I too wanted a ten-inch spiked Mohawk.

It was also around this time that my sinful nature started kicking in. My friends and I were good kids, but we were starting to get a bit mischievous. We would dress in all black and sneak out at night to syrup mailboxes. Somehow our parents always knew what we were up to. One day my dad said to me, "Don't let me catch you putting syrup in mailboxes again." I thought we were as sneaky as could be. How did he know? I have no idea how he found out. Parents know things! Though I knew it was wrong to do, a part of me wanted to fit in. The majority of what I got myself into came from hanging out with the wrong crowd. We weren't all bad. We just had a tendency to do some bad things. We were just kids being kids, but things would get more dangerous down the road. It seemed my friends and I were inseparable, but things are always subject to change.

# ZOMBIE

I 'll never forget my first concert. It was life-changing. The only concert I had seen up to this point was REO Speedwagon, and that was from a distance. It was an outdoor show, and I wasn't inside the actual venue. My dad and I watched from the other side of a park fence where we were hanging out. The first show I attended was White Zombie and the Ramones at the L.C. Walker Arena in Muskegon, Michigan. I first heard of White Zombie on MTV. I would always walk to school in the mornings, which was about a mile hike, but I would spend about a half hour watching MTV before leaving. That way, I could get caught up on the latest music and music videos. This was back when MTV played music, before the era of reality television.

When the music video for "More Human than Human" by White Zombie came on, it immediately had my attention. This was radical, and unlike anything I had ever seen. It was dark, yet it was seductive and attractive. It was dirty and grimy, yet it was appealing. I fell in love with the band. I wanted to be Rob Zombie. I would practice imitating him. I wanted more Zombie! Each morning I waited in anticipation for the video to come on so I could watch it again.

One day, my dad and I were cruising in the car when an ad came on the radio, "White Zombie, *LIVE*, at the L.C. Walker Arena!" The advertisement with the Zombie music in the background had my heart pounding in my chest. Not sure what my dad would say, I didn't say anything to him about wanting to go to the concert. However, I knew that I could not miss it. He was getting ready to drop me off at my mother's house, so I figured I would talk to her about it. My chances of getting the okay from my mom were much higher. My mother agreed to purchase the tickets under the condition that my dad would take me to the concert. Please keep in mind, my parents had no idea who White Zombie was. All they knew was that I was beyond excited about it. Looking back at all the concerts I've been to over the years, I figure I must have a hundred ticket stubs in an envelope somewhere. This concert would be the first of many. It would be the first of many that I would attend. And then there would be the many where I would play. Concerts became a way that our family would bond. Over the years, my parents and I saw everyone from Black Sabbath and Aerosmith to Kiss. The list of bands we saw goes on and on. If there was a show in town, we didn't miss it!

I was only in the sixth grade when my dad and I attended the White Zombie concert. I don't think either of us knew what to expect or what we were really in for. I remember waiting in line outside of the arena. It was February and freezing out. I made sure that we left super early because I wanted to be right up front. I didn't want to miss a thing.

We arrived at the venue several hours before showtime. We were the first ones in line, which ensured that we would get a good spot. At one point, my dad ran across the street to get us some hot chocolate so we could warm up. Once people started arriving and getting in line behind us, I could see a look of concern come across my dad's face that said, "What have we got ourselves into?" Inside the arena, we grabbed a seat up in the bleachers. I remember seeing a couple of kids on the stadium floor playing Hacky Sack. One of them had a yellow Mohawk and wore a sleeveless maroon t-shirt that said Korn on the back of it. A couple of guys sitting behind us also saw the shirt and began discussing this new band that was on the rise. Korn had just started breaking onto the scene at that time and was blowing up quickly. Years later, Head from Korn would come into a relationship with Jesus Christ and write a book titled, *Save Me From Myself.* His story and book became a great inspiration to me. It was one of the tools that God used to give me the strength that I needed when the time came for me to leave the music industry.

I also noticed a smell in the atmosphere of the arena. I liked it and would smell it at rock shows for years to come. I didn't realize what the smell was at that time, but I would later discover that the smell was the combination of alcohol and weed. The show hadn't started yet, and we decided we wanted to be closer. We moved from the bleachers to the floor. The show was general admission. Not only did we move to the floor, but we got right up against the rail. Three guys directly behind us were concerned for us. Apparently, they could tell that we weren't avid concert goers. One of them said, "Listen, when these lights go down, you aren't going to want to be on the floor, let alone up against the rail. It's going to get crazy down here." One of the guys proceeded to tell us how he had been injured from being up front at a Metallica concert. The weight of the crowd pressing against him caused several of his ribs to break against the guardrail.

Neither my dad nor I understood how it could be that bad, so we decided to take our chances. Still, it was kind of them to look out for us. They said that they'd do what they could to hold the crowd back once the show started. The security guard directly in front of us made sure to let us know that if it got too bad and we wanted out, all we had to do was signal him, and he'd pull us right out of there. Then, suddenly, the lights went down. The first act, The Supersuckers, took the stage. It instantly felt like we were in a storm and being tossed around by the waves. People were crowd surfing directly over our heads. The security guards would catch them once they got to the rail.

The three men behind us couldn't hold the crowd back any longer, and I wanted to get out of there. I signaled to the security guard to pull me out. When they pulled me out, I had to walk to the end of the aisle between the stage and the railing where the security guard stood. Once down there, I waited for my dad, but he didn't come out. Minutes later, they pulled him out as well, but I had already exited into the crowd. At this point, I wasn't sure where to go or what to do. It was a scary scene and situation to say the least. As I helplessly stood off to the side of the crowd, a man bent down and asked, "Hey little guy, who are you here with?" I told him that I was with my dad, but we had gotten separated. He picked me up and put me on his shoulders, and I watched most of The Supersuckers' set from that vantage point.

After twenty or thirty minutes, he set me down and told me he had to go. He advised me to stay out of the crowd and off to the side where I'd be alright. He then proceeded to take off into the crowd, where I imagine he got involved in a mosh pit. I began to look up in the bleachers and finally spotted my dad. He saw me and began waving his arms. I ran right up to him. From there, we sat and watched the rest of the show.

The second act to take the stage was the Ramones, with all the original members. At the time, I had absolutely no idea who they were. They were different. I could tell by the response of the crowd that they were a popular band. They were only one of the greatest punk bands ever to walk the face of the earth, if not the greatest. We waited in anticipation of the main act. Suddenly, the lights went down once again, and you could sense a complete change in the atmosphere. There was such anticipation for Zombie. Their introduction built the hype as, one by one, the band members took the stage. It was dark, but there was enough lighting to see the set up. The place erupted. The background of the stage looked like an old pirate ship. Once the band kicked in and the vocals started, Rob came out. There he was. I was staring at Rob Zombie. It was a powerful concert! The show was so good that even my dad enjoyed it. I couldn't believe that I had just seen White Zombie. By the time the show was over, I had officially made up my mind. This is what I was going to do for the rest of my life.

# LET THE BANDS BEGIN

Going to the White Zombie concert opened up a door to the darker side of music for me. I began to develop an interest in the occult. It was one thing that I was going to be a rock star, but I was consumed with the idea that it had to be dark. There seemed to be a sense of power that came with the darkness with which I had become acquainted. I would soon start my first band called Devil. I wanted to be like the rock stars I worshipped. Though only in the sixth grade, I began to draw what would appear to be tattoos all over my hands and arms with a pen. My school folders would become saturated with other band names that I would develop, such as Suicide. My teachers became concerned about me.

I didn't understand the seriousness or the implications of these names at the time. I made a banner that said Devil on it for the purpose of hanging it as my band's backdrop. I knew that we had to have a show and an image. It was time to recruit members. My stepbrother would become my drummer even though he didn't know how to play the drums or even own a set at the time. As far as I was concerned, he could learn how to play, and we could purchase a drum set. We took old clothes and tore holes in them. This was to be one of the things that marked our band.

At the time my hair was shaved on the sides, and I would gel it all towards the middle with the point hanging down my forehead like Glenn Danzig from the Misfits. I even set up a photoshoot for the band. We hung the Devil banner in the background and lit smoke bombs for ambiance. I was all about a show. We had to have a show if we were going to be like Zombie. I only wrote a few songs under this band name. Since my brother never got a drum set and lost interest in the project very quickly, Devil didn't last long. Even though this project seemed to be falling apart, my dream was far from over.

My interest in concerts only increased. The next few concerts I would attend featured bands like Candlebox, Pantera, and Collective Soul. I would later play several shows with Candlebox and Vinnie Paul (now deceased) from Pantera. Concerts and music weren't the only habits I picked up. I also started smoking cigarettes at this time. I remember the very moment I put that first cigarette to my mouth. Everything within me said, "Don't do it." Before long, I would become a Marlboro Man though it was only after some heavy peer pressure from friends that I finally began smoking. I was now doing what I said I would never do. That was to become a theme in my life.

In elementary school, I had signed a waiver in D.A.R.E (Drug Abuse Resistance Education), stating that I would never smoke. I guess they figured if they could keep you from smoking, they could keep you from drugs. I also remember making a promise to my parents that I would never get into drugs. My statement was sincere at the time, but this too wouldn't last. I'll never forget the first time I did cocaine. It was similar to my cigarette experience in the sense of everything in me saying, "Don't do it." I remember the first time I snorted that white powder up my nose. As I was inhaling it, I remember being overcome with a sense of failure and thinking, "How could I let myself get this low?" I felt like a part of my soul was ripped out of me at that moment. It felt like whatever innocence was left had just been lost.

After trying a cigarette for the first time, I started smoking regularly with my friends. We all agreed that we were just doing it for fun and that we could quit anytime we wanted to. At that time, we probably could have, but it would soon become a habit we would not be able to break. To this very day, most of the friends that I started smoking with still smoke. I started smoking Marlboro Lights and worked my way up to Reds. By the time I was in the seventh grade, I was smoking pretty consistently. As a matter of fact, the first thing I would do when I got home from school was step into the backyard for a smoke. My parents weren't home of course.

We would leave the school grounds for lunch or sneak away during school hours when we could to grab a smoke. Once, in junior high, some friends and I snuck down to the basement of the school's gymnasium and followed the tunnel down to the exit. The exit led outside. We cracked the door open just enough to let some fresh air in and the smoke out. We lit up a cigarette and began to pass it around. All of a sudden, the door flew open and there stood our vice principal. There was no way we weren't going to get busted. He just smiled and said, "What's going on in here guys? You know you aren't supposed to be down here. Let's get going and get to class." At this time, one of my friends had the cigarette cupped in his hand to hide it. You could clearly see and smell the smoke. To my amazement, the vice principal never said anything about it. He just let us off the hook. He then walked away, leaving us standing there. We stomped the cigarette out and got to class.

On our lunch break, a group of us would walk over to a local gas station where one of the kids had a connection to buy cigarettes. He'd purchase cigarettes for us, and then we'd all go out back and smoke. One day the cops showed up, and a bunch of kids got busted. I didn't get caught even though I was smoking as well. Later that day, my dad said that my uncle had seen me behind the gas station smoking with a group of kids. I lied my face off stating that he must have been mistaken. The truth was, he had caught me red-handed, but since he didn't have the evidence to prove it, I certainly wasn't going to admit to it.

Later on that year, I'd find myself at parties where I started drinking and smoking weed. Though the drinking and weed, I could do without, my cigarette addiction was getting out of control. I started craving them. I and my friends had a connection who would buy us smokes at that time. I would keep my cigarettes hidden and stashed away. One day, because I had accidentally left a porno video in the VCR before school one morning, my dad went through my room and found my stash. My stash included porn, a carton of cigarettes, and a note from the school that I hid from my parents stating that if I didn't attend summer school, I was going to have to repeat the year again.

Not only was my stash gone, but my dad threw out all of my rock shirts and CDs as well. It was clear where the influence was coming. However, that didn't stop me. The rebel in me simply said, "We just have to start all over again." I ended up going to summer school that year for algebra. I rode my bike back and forth to school, and I guess it's a good thing I went. I had to get through school somehow. Nothing was going to keep me from becoming a rock star. All I wanted to do was play my guitar and rock. I didn't just want to play rock music; I wanted to live the rock and roll lifestyle.

I connected with a friend of mine from school who had a keyboard, and we started writing some songs together. We ended up creating a band called Slight Destiny. This was the closest thing to a real band that I had been a part of up until that point. We wrote some decent songs! At least, we thought we did. My dad was pretty impressed by the tunes that we were coming up with as well. After one of our practices, my dad said, "Man, that was pretty good. That sounded like it could be on the radio." The song he was referring to was called "Demons," and it had an epic intro.

My friend, Gary, and I would meet up early in the mornings and walk to school together, discussing songs, music, and our band's future. Gary was a great artist as well. Looking back now, I think we were both just trying to escape the pain and reality of life. Regardless, I wanted to be a star, and if you wanted to be a star, you had to do what the stars did. Sometimes I would walk to school alone just listening to my Walkman. I would listen to Blind Melon every day. Amazingly, I didn't burn that tape out considering how much I listened to it. I loved that band. If I didn't have Blind Melon in my tape player, I was listening to Metallica's Black Album. This was my favorite Metallica album by far. I loved that it was heavy, yet it was mainstream. Some people said that they had sold out, but I didn't care. I knew what was good when I heard it.

Once in a while, my friend Billy and I would meet up in the morning and walk to school together. We would always stop at the gully on our way to class where we'd smoke a cigarette. We had to get our morning fix before the day started. The gully was a path that crossed through the woods. There was a little bridge over a stream where we'd stop and have a smoke. We would just hang out, smoke, and talk life. Billy and I loved the same music, which is why we got along great. When I stopped at his house in the mornings, he'd usually have one of the Guns N' Roses *Use Your Illusion* albums blaring as he got ready for school. This would get us pumped up for the day. Bands, music, friends, and cigarettes had become my life.

# THE MANSON DAYS

The remake of "Sweet Dreams" by Marilyn Manson had just come out. I didn't know that it was a remake at the time. I would learn that later. When I heard the song, I was hooked. I was an instant Manson fan. He was everything that I loved about rock and roll. He was dirty, rebellious, and most importantly, a showman, or so I thought. As I listened to him, I became more and more interested in the darker things of life. He seemed to have a draw that pulled you in that direction. I needed to wave my Manson banner, so I purchased a Marilyn Manson t-shirt that said "Sweet Dreams" on the back of it. I also bought a White Zombie t-shirt that displayed the number 666 on its back.

I soon purchased the album *Smells Like Children* by Marilyn Manson. If the title doesn't say evil, then I don't know what does. After purchasing *Smells Like Children,* I also purchased their debut album titled, *Portrait of an American Family.* Everything about this man and his band was pure evil. It was darker than anything else I had encountered up to this point, yet for some reason, I wanted more of it. I didn't just become a Manson fan; I became a diehard fan. At thirteen, I started wearing black lipstick, powdering my face white, and wearing eyeliner and mascara. I would put symbolic markings on my face to mimic the Manson family, although I had no idea what the symbols meant. I would even draw stitching over my eyebrows with eyeliner.

To me, all this was nothing more than a form of self-expression. I was expressing who it was I followed by being like Manson. A disciple always looks like his master. Though it was dark, very dark, and I did not understand the implications of what I was doing, I saw this as nothing more than harmless entertainment. It got to the point where I started wearing dresses and ripped nylon leggings on my arms. This is how I would go out in public. I was all in. One dress, in particular, was my favorite. It was a long red dress that I took from my mother's closet. I would wear that along with nylons and combat boots. To me, this was the ultimate expression of rock and roll. It didn't get any heavier than this. If you wanted to know whether I had been smoking or not, all you had to do was look for the cigarette butts with the black lipstick on them.

My life got much darker during the Manson era. A friend of mine and I graffitied one of my bedroom walls. We covered it with anarchy symbols, band names, and other demonic stuff. We also took a Lisa Simpson doll that I had and turned her into a voodoo doll. We lit her on fire, spray painted her and put a bunch of pins in her head. She hung around for a while. I'm not sure whatever happened to Lazarus Lisa, but she must have gotten tossed out at some point.

One night, my friend Malcolm came over to hang out. We smoked some cigarettes and listened to rock music in my bedroom. He and I would get together a lot since we were super close friends. We would sit next to my bedroom window with it cracked open so that the smoke would blow directly out of it. We didn't want my mom to catch on to what we were doing. We would put our cigarettes out and toss them right outside the window into the backyard. Malcolm was staying over, and as we were getting ready for bed, I was staring at my bedroom window trying to figure out what the orange glow reflecting off of it was.

Suddenly it dawned on me, "Fire!" Malcolm and I ran out of the house as fast as we could to see what was going on. We discovered that a portion of the house outside of my bedroom window was on fire. Apparently, one of the cigarettes hadn't been put all the way out. Lucky for us, there was a hose right around the corner. As if we were a couple of highly trained firemen, we cranked the water faucet on and put the fire out. Had I not caught a glimpse of that orange glow when I did, our house could have easily burned down. Worse yet, it could have burned down with us in it. Even then, God was looking out for my family and for me.

Right when I thought Manson couldn't get any darker, their second studio album *Antichrist Superstar* came out. Its first single was titled "The Beautiful People." I found out that Manson was coming to Michigan, and I told my mother that we had to go to this concert. I remember her saying, "Are you sure you want to go to that concert?" It was as if she knew something that I didn't. I was adamant, and so we did. From the moment we pulled into the parking lot, I could feel that something was off. There was something here that I hadn't felt at any other concert before. This was spiritual warfare to the max. People were picketing the concert and protesters heckling the people in line. There were also large groups of Christians praying at various spots in the parking lot. I watched a group of Christians with one girl who had stepped out of line to receive prayer from them. She was crying. I didn't understand what was happening at the time, but she was being touched by the Spirit of God. I thought I was just going to another show. I had bit off more than I could chew.

People in line were decked out in black makeup, robes, and other types of dark garments. Once inside, we were immediately seated. The guy sitting directly behind us was smoking a massive joint and had an upside-down cross painted on his forehead. The scene around us was overwhelming. I was almost afraid to move. We saw a woman walking around on the floor with a baby strapped to her back. Even the gentleman behind us said, "Man, that's just wrong." Before the show started, they had some creepy children's music playing over the P.A. system. This was about as demonic as it got. I went down on the floor for a moment only to run right back up to my seat. Everyone seemed drugged out and unfriendly. You could feel the presence of evil in this arena. It just didn't feel safe on the floor. The band Helmet and a female cello quartet opened the show, but when Manson came out, it was unlike anything I had ever seen or experienced before. This was different. It was as if all hell broke loose, literally.

I remember the lights going down in the arena and the stage curtains gradually pulling back. Manson was dressed in a white corset and had some sort of a cup on. Whatever he was wearing, it wasn't much. He came walking down what appeared to be the staircase to a Catholic Church. It was a very solemn and dark intro. Once the band kicked in, it was complete chaos in that place. His movements were extremely creepy. At one point, he had the entire crowd spit on him as he wiped his posterior with the American flag. During the show, a tornado touched down, and the authorities wanted to stop the show, but Manson refused. The show went on. They played "Sweet Dreams" in the dark with nothing but a garage light hanging from the lighting fixtures for the first part of the song. All you could see was his face lit by the garage light. Once the whole band kicked in, he smashed the garage light and began to cut himself with the broken shards of glass. He had to step off stage, get bandaged up, and then come back out.

I had never seen a show that took an intermission before, but they did. Maybe it was due to his bleeding. When they came back on after about a fifteen-minute intermission, they had the stage set up to look like Nazi Germany, and he was singing from behind a podium. The band members all had military helmets on. They had huge red banners that draped down each side of the stage with the graphic from the *Antichrist Superstar* album on them. As he stood behind the podium, moving in a contorted type manner, he began to rip pages out of a Bible and throw them into the crowd. At one point, he stopped the set and said, "Turn the house lights on! I want everyone to shout and show those people outside how much power is in this room!" The place erupted with a loud roar. The people that he had been referring to were the Christians outside of the arena praying. I must add, the most silent prayer of any Christian will always be stronger than the devil's loudest roar.

When we left the show, I was speechless. I was stunned and reticent. I didn't have anything to say. I had been to many rock concerts up to this point, but this was something different. It didn't feel like I left a rock concert; it felt more like I had just left a war zone, and I had. The battle between darkness and light was very evident. It's as if the people on the inside of the building were at war with those outside of it. I would come to understand, much later in life, what the Apostle Paul wrote in a letter to the church at Ephesus in chapter six, verse 12 (KJV): "For we wrestle not against flesh and blood, but against principalities, against powers, against rulers of the darkness of this world, against spiritual wickedness in high places." That night, though, I had no words to describe what I had experienced in that "concert."

Despite the concert, I continued to be a Manson supporter and continued to wear all his gear. This would cause conflict for me at school. In one instance, a teacher told me that if I wanted to stay in his classroom, I had to turn my Manson shirt inside out. On the front of the shirt, it said "See no truth, hear no truth, speak no truth," and the back of the shirt said, "Believe," with the l, i, and e highlighted to spell out the word lie. It didn't bother me to do so, but a student fought against the teacher for me and won my case. The teacher finally agreed to let me wear the shirt.

On another occasion, I came to school decked out in all my Manson gear. I had the dress on and the whole nine yards. We were just starting class when the teacher looked at me and said, "Is it Halloween?" As everyone laughed, he said, "No, seriously, did I miss it?" It was near the end of October. When I said it wasn't, he asked me to wash my makeup off as it was a distraction to his class. His student assistant fought for me in this case and persuaded the teacher to allow me to leave it on, but by that point, I had already washed it off. I wasn't doing this to rebel or to cause trouble. To me, this was an expression of the music that I loved and made.

Music was truly an expression to me and was something that I was deeply passionate about and loved. I didn't understand the spiritual side of it, and how could I? To me, this was about achieving my goals and my dreams. I just wanted to be a rock star. My friends and I would always talk about what life would be like once I got famous. It was like we knew it was going to happen; it was just a matter of time.

At this point, I had gotten much better musically and had upgraded my gear. My mother saw that I was still serious about music and staying the course, so she took me to Rick's one day to potentially get me a new guitar. I went into the store and began checking out the guitars. I loved trying out their guitars just to show off. I was a huge Dimebag Darrell fan (Pantera's guitarist), and because he played a Washburn that meant that I had to play a Washburn. Later in life, I would end up endorsed by Dean and playing his line of guitars. I picked out this beautiful burgundy red Sammy Hagar Cabo Wabo edition Washburn. My mother ended up buying it for me as a gift. This was not easy for her to do as we didn't have the money for it. It was no cheap instrument. It was well over $1,000.00. But I will say this, she could not have given me a better gift. I played that guitar non-stop. I absolutely loved it. That guitar would be my primary axe (guitar) for a while, and Washburn would become my guitar of choice because of Darrell.

Had my mom not supported me the way that she did, I never would have had the success that I had. She was more than a supporter; she was truly my best friend. I loved spending time with her and just talking about life. In the mornings, before school, we would sit and have coffee together and chat. I would head to school, and she would head to work. She'd even take time to braid my hair for me as it was quite long during this period.

My mom and I really connected. Sometimes in the morning, I would put a shot of Bailey's Original Irish Cream liqueur in my coffee not thinking anything about it. I used it as a creamer. I didn't think too much of it until my mom came home one day reeking of booze. I said, "Have you been drinking?" She said, "Just a little Bailey's in my coffee!" I must have gone to school smelling like that!

You could really smell it! I'm surprised I never got questioned by a professor. All it took was one shot to smell like a liquor cabinet. And that was aside from the fact that I also reeked from the cigarettes smoked on my way to school every morning. Sometimes my friends and I would try to cover it up by spraying cologne on ourselves, but that never worked! We just ended up smelling like Tommy Hilfiger and smoke!

As much as my mother and I got along, I was a difficult kid to deal with. I wasn't a bad kid, just very difficult at times. Getting me up for school was a chore for her. I hated waking up in the mornings, so much so that one day my mom pinned a magazine ad that she had found to my bedroom door. It was a picture of a little boy in a lion outfit crying, and it said, "One cranky king." That was me. I was definitely cranky in the mornings, to say the least.

One morning, after several attempts by my mother to get me out of bed, I finally woke up and made my way to the kitchen. I sat down in one of our kitchen chairs leaning back against the wall. I was still trying to open my eyes. Suddenly, I sneezed. My mother looked over at me and said, "Oh! God bless you!" I snapped back at her, "Don't bless me!" She politely said, "I didn't bless you. I said, God bless you." I looked at her with an evil little smirk on my face and cursed the name of God. I won't repeat what I said. Ironically, in that moment, a pan that was hanging on the wall behind me fell off its hook hitting and bouncing off my head. The average person might write this off as a coincidence, but that pan had been hanging there for years, and it had never fallen off the hook before. I'm sure there was an angel there to slide it off the hook when I opened my mouth against God. I just sat there in surprise. My mother looked at me, smiled, and said, "You better watch what you say about God."

# GASOLINE & HELL

I may have started with drinking and smoking cigarettes, but I got to a point when that just wasn't cutting it anymore. Weed wasn't cutting it either. I was looking for something more. I was never a big fan of weed anyway. I didn't care for how it made me feel. And my friends and I were adrenaline and trouble junkies, always looking for that next big rush. I had started hanging out with this kid named Lenny. Lenny and I would find ourselves getting into trouble regularly. One winter day, we went so far as to steal a liquor bottle from a local house knowing that no one was home. We took the bottle of liquor sledding with us and crushed the entire thing. Sledding would never be the same again.

One day Lenny suggested that we should huff gasoline. He said he had seen a documentary about it on television and that he wanted to try it. I was in, yet I was hesitant because we both understood that we could die from doing this. That was the point of the documentary. It was not encouraging it; it was bringing awareness to the problem. Despite the hesitancy, we did it. Lenny and I would often getaway to a secret place where it was just him and me, and we would huff and trip for hours. We would see hallucinations as we huffed, which is one of the primary reasons we wanted to do it. One time we were huffing in a house when I turned and saw a liquid bomb with a timer set to go off. I shouted, "It's gonna blow!" Lenny responded, "What's gonna blow?" Experiences like this would take place regularly as we huffed. I guess that's what kept us coming back for more.

One time while I was tripping, I had become a molecule on the inside of my lip. In my hallucination, which seemed completely real at the time, I walked around the corner of my lip and saw a big mean-looking molecule. That's when I shouted out loud, "A molecule!" Lenny responded, "Oh no, the big bad molecule!" He was laughing hysterically. These trips or hallucinations seemed so real. Had it not been for the mercy and grace of God on my life, I would not be here today. During one of our gas huffing episodes, I would have an experience that would change my life forever. I wouldn't completely understand or make sense of this experience until further down the road.

Lenny and I had gotten together one day to huff gasoline as we usually did. This day would be different, very different. I put my mouth to the gas can and inhaled. I never had a chance to exhale; I was gone. Suddenly, I was in a different location. It was dark. It was very dark. It was darker than any darkness I had ever seen before. It was so dark that it was as if the darkness were alive. I was sitting on what felt like a concrete slab, hugging my knees, with my back pressed up against a wall. I was rocking back and forth in confusion trying to figure out where I was. I did not know where I was nor how I had gotten there. What was this place?

Though I couldn't see, I could feel my clothes. I had the same clothes on. It was as if I had simply teleported into a different dimension. I was truly afraid to move. I couldn't see my hand directly in front of my face, let alone ten feet in front of me. For all I knew, I could have been on the edge of a cliff. I just sat there trying to figure this whole thing out. Yet, I began to hear whispers out in the distant darkness. Sitting in this place of nothingness, I shouted, "Hello! Is there anybody there?!" The word "there" just seemed to echo out into the hollowness of nothing. I shouted a second time, "Hello! Is there anyone there?!" That last word would echo with each call.

Finally, I heard a voice, and it stirred me. I pressed up against the wall. "Who's there?" I said, completely startled. Then I heard the voice calling for me again. I recognized it. It was Lenny. I responded, "Lenny, is that you? What are you doing here?" At that point, my eyes opened only to find Lenny standing over me and shaking me. I just looked at him and asked, "What happened?" He said, "You passed out. You fell over. You started turning purple. I thought you were dead!" In reality, I was dead. I had died and left my body, yet when you leave your body, you are still in your body. I had transported to a new location. The Apostle Paul says in 2 Corinthians 5:8, "We are of good courage, I say, and prefer rather to be absent out of the body and to be at home with the Lord" (NASB). I was absent from this natural realm alright, but I wasn't at home with the Lord. I did not know Him. I had never made Jesus, who is the only way to Heaven, the Lord of my life.

In John 14:6, Jesus said, "I am the way, and the truth, and the life; no one comes to the Father but through Me" (NASB). And regarding the darkness, Jesus made a statement in Matthew 25:30 that I experienced. He said, "And throw that worthless servant outside, into the darkness, where there will be weeping and gnashing of teeth" (NIV). We usually connect Hell with fire, and ultimately, yes, that's what it is. "Then death and Hades were thrown into the lake of fire. The lake of fire is the second death" (Revelation 20:14, NIV). But we shouldn't miss what Jesus said. Prior to the Lake of Fire, a person will be in Hell, which is a place of outer darkness and torment. Ultimately, it's a place where those who rejected Christ will suffer and burn forever.

Jesus stated that it is a place, "Where their worm does not die and the fire is not quenched" (Mark 9:48, ESV). In other words, it is eternal. There is no end to the torment. Without a doubt, at thirteen years old, I had died and gone to Hell. Shortly after that experience, Lenny and I quit huffing gasoline. We realized that maybe it wasn't such a good idea after all.

Lenny and I remained close friends. We would soon have our first backstage concert experience together. Lenny scored tickets for us to go and see Buckcherry and Monster Magnet. Later in life, I would end up touring with Buckcherry. We weren't even able to drive yet; we were still in junior high school at this time. We had gotten dropped off at the show. I was no stranger to this arena as I had seen many rock shows there before. To my surprise, the place was pretty empty. For a stadium that held ten thousand people, they would have been lucky if there were one hundred in attendance, no exaggeration.

The show hadn't started yet, so Lenny and I went down on the floor. A bunch of old '80s rockers surrounded us. Lenny had gone to the restroom and come back. Upon his return, he was super excited. "Bro, I think I just scored us some backstage passes," he said. I thought, "What?!" On his way to the restroom, he had run into a guy from one of the local radio stations who had apparently stopped him searching for weed, but Lenny didn't have any weed on him. The guy from the station said, "If you can get me some weed, I will trade you a couple of backstage passes for it." Why he propositioned a thirteen-year-old to fulfill this mission will always be beyond me, but it happened. I guess he figured a young kid at a rock concert probably smoked, and he was right. He told us that he would announce us as the winners for the drawing of the passes and that we could come and pick them up. Lenny quickly ran across the street to a payphone and made a call. We didn't have cell phones at that time. He contacted one of his connections, who was able to drop off the goods. Sure enough, we made the trade. Lenny scored the disc jockey some weed, and the disc jockey honored his word by calling us up as the winners of the passes. We ran right up to the booth to claim our prize.

The show itself wasn't bad, but I had seen better. Either way, we had a great time. I was excited to hear "Space Lord" by Monster Magnet and "Lit Up" by Buckcherry. The passes that we ended up with were actually "meet and greet" passes for Monster Magnet. I ended up getting a business card from their tour manager, who also worked for a label at the time. For years, I would stay in touch with him sending him recordings of different projects I was part of and getting his input. This was another level for me; I had never been backstage before. We were just a couple of junior high school kids.

I really wanted to see the Buckcherry guys. Though I didn't see them, Lenny caught a glimpse of a member of Buckcherry doing a keg stand in a dressing room full of people. It was cool getting to meet real rock stars. These were some true party bands. While a member of one of the bands from the evening was autographing my ticket stub for me, he asked me to hold his drink. I asked, "Can I take a swig?" He looked around the room and then kind of nodded at me as if to say, "Go ahead!" A swig I took! It was Jack and Coke. Not only would I have many more backstage experiences in my life, but they would be taking place in my dressing room. This was the life! I was determined to make it. I had determined in my heart that I was going to be a rock star, and nothing was going to stop me. I was on a mission.

It seemed like I was always in the process of either putting a band together or joining one. I would see this guy around school from time to time, who was a true rocker. He was in high school while I was still in junior high. I knew he was the real deal. I would see him drive onto the school grounds in the morning in his black van with the music cranked up. He had band stickers of all of the different bands that I loved all over his vehicle. He usually had shades on, and he had long hair. There was no way he could have that vibe and not actually play. I always wanted to talk to him because he seemed so cool.

Chris was his name. It turns out that he was a musician and had a band. They were looking for a lead guitarist. At the time, they were just a trio consisting of a bassist, drummer, and rhythm guitarist. Chris was the guitarist. They could play, though; that was for sure! These guys had the look, the vibe, the skill, and most importantly, they had the gear. We'd be rock stars in no time. After just a short audition, I was in. I loved plugging into the Marshall stacks they had. I would plug into that thing and just let it rip. Usually, when we got together, we would just jam on old Metallica and Black Sabbath riffs.

The band had one problem. We didn't have a singer. Eventually, I'd bring my friend, Chad, in to be our vocalist. Chad was a kid I knew from school. We never really did record anything, but we would tear it up rocking out in the garage. We would have everything up so loud that I'm sure the entire neighborhood could hear us. On one occasion, we had an officer show up due to a noise complaint. He spent most of his time talking to us about a band that he was in when he was younger. He just told us to turn it down and left it at that. We wanted it loud because we wanted to be heard. Wasn't that the point?

I'll never forget our first and only show. It was in the backyard of Chad's parents' house. The backyard was more like a small field. We had access to a hay trailer that served as our stage. It was only big enough for our gear and the band. In our minds, we were already rock stars. This was going to be the show of our lives. We even had an area that we used as a backstage. It was in the basement of Chad's dad's garage, which was directly behind the hay trailer; I mean the stage. We ended up completely botching the show. Afterward, our drummer was so mad that he walked around our "dressing room" kicking stuff. The truth is, we weren't prepared for it. What worked in the basement didn't cut it on the stage. With a little more work, we probably could have been a great band, but the band was short-lived after that show.

# THE SUPERNATURAL

The supernatural is something that has always pulled at me. I've always found it to be fascinating, and maybe that's why I've experienced so much of it. If there was anything that involved tapping into the unseen realm, I was into it. I didn't know what I was getting into at the time or even understand it, but the unseen realm would become an integral part of my life. I was searching for the beyond. I knew that there had to be more than what we could see. I believed in supernatural manifestations. In my hunger for more of the unseen, I even gave using a Ouija board a whirl, but it did not work at that time. What I was truly longing for was God; I just didn't know it yet.

My interest in the paranormal was deep. It started at a young age for me. I was just a little kid when I started getting into horror films. I was about four years old the first time I saw *Nightmare on Elm Street.* It really opened me up to a spirit of fear. I couldn't sleep at night after watching that film. I would lie in bed waiting for Freddy to come through the door at any moment. Horror films taught me about the occult and the demonic realm. I didn't know it at the time, but I was being trained and brainwashed by watching these films.

I became a horror film fanatic. I had quite a collection of VHS tapes I had recorded including such films as, *Nightmare on Elm Street* and *Friday the 13th.* These films were nothing more than entertainment to me; at least, that's what I thought. Part of the reason I liked the group White Zombie so much was that they had a horror film aura about them. I would later get into the films that Rob Zombie would direct such as, *House of a 1,000 Corpses* and *The Devil's Rejects.*

What I did not know was that spirits operated through film. I would later learn this firsthand, which is partially why I was so interested in films dealing with the paranormal. *Paranormal Activity* was more than a movie title to me. It would become a regular part of my life. I was no stranger to spiritual activity. I knew one thing for sure; though I couldn't see it, there was a spiritual realm that existed beyond the natural one that I could see. For instance, once as a child, I could hear someone going through my toys in the next room. They were digging through my toy box; only there was no one in the room. It was terrifying.

I used to have a Halloween doll that was a witch. When you shook it, it would start laughing. This was a battery-operated doll. One time I heard it going off by itself, laughing in the other room. It should not have been going off without someone activating it. I stood frozen for a minute before moving. When I went and checked on it, not only would it not stop laughing, but I noticed that it had no batteries in it. These types of experiences caused me to dig deeper. It would have been impossible for me to be an atheist. Even though I didn't understand what was happening, it was tough to deny the reality of the supernatural realm.

I didn't know much about religion. I had only been to church a couple of times as a kid. What intrigued me was Islam. I was around it a lot since I had spent so much time in Turkey. Turkey is 99.9 percent Islamic. The mosques seemed to grab your attention everywhere you went. You could hear the "Call to Prayer" sounding from them all over the city. As kids in Turkey, we spent most of our time at the beach. We were hardly ever inside, only to eat or sleep. My grandmother would tell us, "When you hear the 'Call to Prayer' going off, it's time to come in for dinner." So when we heard it, we would head right home.

Though Islam had an intriguing element to it, I didn't understand it at all. One time I wiped my feet off on a friend's grandfather's prayer rug as I thought it was the welcome mat to the house. He had left it right inside the front door where he had been praying. He wasn't too happy with me to say the least. Later, at the age of fifteen, I ordered and read through the Quran in my search for truth. I longed for truth. I longed for God. I believed in Him, and I wanted to know Him. The Old Testament prophet Jeremiah wrote, "You will seek Me and find Me when you seek Me with all your heart" (Jeremiah 29:13, NIV). I knew God existed, but there were so many different religions. How could I know who the true God was? Which religion was the truth?

I read the Quran cover to cover in just a few days. To my surprise, it did not satisfy my quest for God. It did not quench the thirst that was on the inside of me. It had no life to it. I knew that this could not be The Book. This was not what I was looking for. The Book of the Living God that I was looking for had life to it, and I knew this in my spirit. I was always seeking. Later on, during my Pop Evil days, I would pick up the Book of Mormon just to check it out. I had plenty of time to read while we were traveling. In the early days, we traveled in a Denali. Sitting in the back of the vehicle,

I randomly opened The Book of Mormon up to page 111. At that moment, I looked up and noticed that we were passing the 111-mile marker. Was this a coincidence? There are no coincidences. These are what I call God winks. God was always trying to get my attention. Experiences like this one happened all the time. It was as if God was saying, "I am with you." I never did make it more than a few pages through the Book of Mormon. Like the Quran, the book had no life.

The supernatural became my new normal. A few years down the road, I reconnected with a girl that I had previously dated only to find out that she had just gotten out of an abusive relationship. Apparently, the guy that she was with had been locked up and was about to get out of jail. She was absolutely terrified. She needed a new lock for her house, but she did not have the money for one. One day I prayed, "God, you have to do something." I received a clear response. God said, "No, you have to do something, and I'm going to help you do it." When He spoke that, it was as if the plan was downloaded into my spirit, and I knew exactly what I had to do.

I was just a young man, and I didn't have much cash at the time. God spoke to me that I was to take the money that I did have, and I was to buy this young lady a new lock. I withdrew the twenty dollars I had in my bank account and added to it change that I had saved up in a jar. Unbelievably, the twenty dollars combined with the change equaled the lock's price, down to the penny. God is constantly speaking. The question is, are we listening?

Again, there are no coincidences. We should not write God moments off as anything other than God. He is continually trying to get our attention. As much as I knew God existed, I didn't know who He was. I wanted to know Him. I would later learn that I, like all believers, was meant to be the hands and feet of Christ in this world.

As much as these cool God moments would take place in my life, so would encounters with the demonic realm. When you are tuned into the supernatural, you will be exposed to both ends of the spectrum. Once, at eighteen, I was with a girl in my room. It was dark other than a candle we had lit. Suddenly, this presence of terror took over the atmosphere. We both became very aware of it. As we looked at each other, the candle began to slowly go out, until we were both sitting there in the pitch-black darkness. It was silent. All I could hear was our heavy breathing and the sound of our hearts beating in our chests. We didn't move; we just sat there in the dark. As we were sitting and listening, the clock in the room began to tick. That might not seem so strange except for the fact that the clock, like my old Halloween doll, did not have batteries in it.

I was acutely aware that the presence of God was operating in my life. But, I was also aware that there was something very evil and strange lurking about as well. I was no stranger to the supernatural, and by supernatural I simply mean the realm beyond the veil of what we can see. There was a war that was taking place for my life, and it was evident. The unseen realm was very real to me. In fact, it was more real than the natural realm that I could see. One time, I came home from school and went into the bathroom where I noticed the lights were flickering. It was as if someone was letting me know, "We are here." This often happened as I entered different rooms. I knew that it was a form of communication. I understood this in my spirit. There was only one way to find out if something or someone was there truly, and that was to ask it.

I went out into the kitchen of our house and asked this simple question, "If there's someone there, can you prove it to me by dimming the lights?" We had a chandelier style light that hung over our kitchen table. The light was completely turned up. Upon asking my question, it dimmed all the way down and then came back up. Just to rule out any coincidences, I asked it a second time, "If there's someone there, could you dim the lights for me one more time?" The lights dimmed all the way down and then came back up. Not only was the supernatural normal for me, but it would become an integral part of my life.

# THE JAM RYDER BAND

By the time ninth grade came along, I had shoulder-length brown hair, wore a leather jacket and had quite the collection of Chuck Taylor shoes. Sometimes I would mismatch different colored shoes just to be creative. For example, I would wear one green shoe and one blue one. They were the same shoe, just different colors. One night I ended up in the police station for underage drinking, and the guy sitting next to me looked at my feet and, perplexed, asked, "Do you have two different color shoes on?" He was relieved to find out that I did. He had taken a hit of acid and was not excited about the idea of tripping out in the police station. I was a colorful character, and whatever rock and roll was, I wanted to live and be that.

My transition from junior high to high school brought with it many new friends and adventures. I would meet an entirely new group of kids whom I had never known before. It was a bit of a rough transition, but many of the high schoolers would end up becoming good friends of mine. I didn't seem to fit into any one particular group, but I got along with everybody. It didn't matter what clique you belonged to; I would find a way to relate and connect with you.

I would soon meet a group that would become my regular crew. We were like a gang. One day on my way home from school, I stopped in the Gully to have a smoke. This was my after-school routine. A few minutes later, a young man approached me asking if he could bum a cigarette. His name was Grisham. I bargained with him. I told him that I would bum him a smoke if he would buy me a pack. He made a counteroffer and said that he would buy me a pack if I would split it with him.

Needless to say, Grisham and his group became my friends. We were good kids at heart, but boy, we liked to get into trouble. Grisham had an old car that was the size of a boat in which the gang and I would cruise around. Matter of fact, we would take it down to the local strip where all the rich kids would show off their fancy cars. We would drive the strip in our busted up looking beater hollering at all the girls. Shockingly, this seemed to work.

The car did not have a stereo system in it or windshield wipers that worked, but this vehicle was completely rigged out. They had tied rope to the wiper blades that would reach the inside of the car so that when it would rain, the driver would pull the rope in one direction to pull the wiper blades up, and the front seat passenger would pull them in the opposite direction to bring them back down. Because this classic had no stereo in it, we had a boom box that we kept in the back window that was battery operated, of course. We would have that thing blaring, usually playing Static-X.

One time we went cruising and decided to smash mailboxes. We had a baseball bat that we kept in the trunk for such occasions as these. Life with the "Red Crew," as I called them, was quite the life. We were all about partying, good times, and getting into trouble. We lived in a small town, so there wasn't much to do. Finding trouble to get into only seemed appropriate, what I liked to call harmless fun.

One time the Red Crew dressed up in all black and headed downtown on foot. It was a weeknight when no one else was around. We walked around until we spotted a cop. Once we saw him and acknowledged that he saw us, we all split up and ran in different directions. Though we hadn't done anything wrong, this made it look like we were up to no good and gave the cop a reason to come after us. I guess it gave both us and the cop something to do on a quiet small-town night. The cop singled a few of us out and chased after us, and we spent the next hour or so running through town ducking and dodging police officers. It was a blast—what a way to pass the time.

Sometimes we'd all get together and play "Capture the Flag" between neighborhood yards as well. Our days were filled with smoking, drinking, and living our lives to the fullest capacity that we knew how. One of the kids in the Red Crew could throw down. We'll call him the Hammer. He could fight. He had such a reputation that no one messed with him. To this day, he has never lost a fight. That's including local competitions he entered as well as boxing matches he got into in the military. The Hammer would serve in the U.S. Army, which included many tours of duty in hostile nations. He was always in beast mode. It was good to have someone like this on your side. Even when he was off at war, I always knew he'd be fine. He was a soldier before he ever enlisted. He had a type of "David spirit" on him. He was such an unstoppable force to reckon with. If there was anyone I feared for, it was his enemies, not him. I knew the Hammer would take them out.

Later on, during my Pop Evil days, I would hang out with the Red Crew from time to time when I was back in town from being on tour. One night a few of us went out to a local bar, and one guy started mouthing off to me because of who I was. Before I could even say anything, the Hammer said to me, "I'll handle it." Nobody messed with him because of his reputation. I watched as he went over to the guy, put his arm around him, and whispered something in his ear. Whatever he said seemed to work because from that point on, the guy left us alone. We had some drinks, caught up like old times, and shot some pool. I later asked the Hammer what he said to the guy to quiet him up. He said, "I told him if he opened his mouth again, I was going make him eat that beer bottle," and he would have. We were just the type of crew that you didn't mess with.

At this point, I didn't have a band. I was in ninth grade. Though I wasn't in a band, I still played my guitar for hours a day. It was all that I did. But I didn't like being without a band because I knew it would take a band to make it. This wasn't something that I was called to do alone. For me to get to where I wanted to be in the music industry, I would need to surround myself with like-minded musicians. I was always on the lookout for other players. One day I saw an ad on the bulletin board in the back of a music store. Whoever posted it had listed their influences and stated that they were looking for a lead guitar player for their four-piece band which included a drummer, rhythm guitarist, bass player, and a female vocalist. They had left their phone number at the bottom of the advertisement.

Since I didn't have a band at the time, I thought it was worth checking this one out. I auditioned for them and, I can't say I was surprised, they loved me. Their vocalist could sing; she could tear up some Journey! There were a few songs we covered at the time, including "Don't Stop Believing" by Journey, and "What's Up?" by 4 Non Blondes. I was fifteen years old at that time.

One night, we all went out to an open mic and got up and played a few songs. The crowd loved us. It was funny because a relative of mine was there. He saw me and said, "Tony? What are you doing here?" It's not often that you see a fifteen-year-old in a bar. However, if I was going to make it, I needed a platform. The female vocalist didn't last too long, and with her departure, the guys wanted to know if I still wanted to get together and jam out with them. We ended up calling ourselves The Jam Ryder Band. I would stay with them on the weekends, and we would spend that time jamming out. One Friday night, one of the members said to me, "Listen, we need you to know something about us. We smoke pot. If this is something that you are not comfortable with, we totally understand." I responded, "It's no problem; I smoke pot too!" Each band member looked at each other as if to say, "Really?" It's not what they expected to come out of the mouth of this fifteen-year-old. I answered, "Yes really, I've been smoking pot for years!" This changed the entire dynamic of the band.

From that day forward, our jam sessions became a smoking frenzy. They just wanted to make sure that they weren't pressuring me into anything and that I was doing this of my own accord. We would get smoked out and jam for hours. There are recordings of these sessions somewhere. We would just play and play as if we were caught up in some kind of a trance. When we took a break from playing, it was either to listen to some tunes or to pack another bowl. Either way, our little smoke breaks opened me up to a whole new world of music.

I had always been a metal guy, but these guys turned me onto some blues. They could not believe that I hadn't heard of a lot of the artists they were mentioning. They turned me onto guys like Hendrix, Stevie Ray Vaughan, the Vaughn Brothers, and many other great blues players. We would even spend much time listening to the Allman Brothers and the Dave Matthews Band. Dickey Betts of The Allman Brothers Band was one of their favorite guitar players, and he was good indeed. One time, we all went to a Dave Matthews concert together. We got so ripped before going in that we were completely stoned out of our minds. Getting turned onto blues music during this time, I became a huge Kenny Wayne Shepherd fan; I would go and see him open up for Aerosmith. I had some wild times with this band. Other than a few open mics, we never played out. We didn't even officially have any songs. We were just a jam band. Though I didn't get stage experience with them, I learned a lot about music and improv playing.

One thing that surprised me about them was that they really seemed to believe in God despite their hippy lifestyle. One evening I brought an Extreme album over because I wanted them to check it out. Nuno Bettencourt was a phenomenal guitar player. The lyrics to one of the songs questioned whether God made man or was it man who made God. This seemed to deeply offend them. They got a Bible out and began reading the book of Romans to me. We were baked out of our minds at the moment which didn't help. To be honest with you, I didn't even see it coming. Even then, seeds were being planted into my life. It was interesting. This was life for us. We would get as baked as we could, and we would play 'till we had nothing left to give.

One band, they turned me onto was Pink Floyd. *Dark Side of the Moon* soon became one of my all-time favorite albums. The more I got into Pink Floyd, the more I appreciated what they did. The guitar playing was so good, so tasteful. It was music that you could feel. Getting high and listening to Pink Floyd was somewhat of a spiritual experience. One night I took my experience with Pink Floyd to another level. I had heard that *Dark Side of the Moon* correlated with the movie *The Wizard of Oz*. In other words, if you started the album at a specific point before the movie started, it would parallel the entire film. You had to turn the volume off on the movie and crank the Pink Floyd album up. Not only did I get into the Floyd/Oz combo, but I would watch it while high on shrooms. The music went right along with the movie. It was amazing. Watching it sober was cool enough, but being high took it to another level. This would end up becoming a pastime that I would often share with friends.

One day, the Jam Ryder Band just seemed to come to an end. We stopped connecting. Our jam sessions faded away.

# BIDTTER ECSTASY

I just wanted to be playing in a band. As far as I was concerned, if I wasn't engaged in a project, then I wasn't actively moving forward. I was determined to reach my goal, so I had to remain active. Ted would still have me on stage to play with his band during shows. He was a great guitar instructor. I was still taking lessons from him at that time. I loved watching his band. My favorite song they covered was "Got No Shame" by a band called Brother Cane. When I would go on stage with them, I would play "Where the River Flows," a song by Collective Soul. The only other song I ever played with them was a song by Creed.

Watching Ted play was one of the highlights of my life. I just loved being around him. He was a great guitar player. I had more time to spend with him after my departure from the Jam Ryder Band. At one point, I ended up playing guitar for a hip hop studio in the hood. That was an interesting time. I enjoyed rap and hip hop, especially if it had a beat I could groove and drop some riffs to. I was heavily into Twiztid, but I also liked some Cypress Hill, Dre, and Snoop. My taste included more than just metal. Since I was only fifteen and couldn't drive, I would have to catch rides to the rap studio. Deep down, I loved rap.

Once I started getting into the bar scene, I would often play at a rock club that was adjacent to a night club. Between our sets, I would go next door to the night club. You could usually find me on the dance floor busting a move or otherwise at the bar getting a shot. I loved dancing. If they were playing Usher's "Yeah!" or "California Love" by 2Pac, it was on. This was just another way for me to pick up girls. I would be playing rock songs in one club, then cutting a rug to some hip hop in the other. After a few sessions in the hip hop studio, I realized that it wasn't for me. As much as I enjoyed rap, I was a rock guitarist and that needed to be my focal point, so I got back on track with that.

The supernatural occurrences continued. I didn't understand them, but things would happen from time to time. When I would come home from school, often the first thing I would do was take a nap. One day I got home from school, and I set my backpack down in the living room. I planned on napping on the couch as I often did. As I lay there, I couldn't help but notice the music that was playing in my head. At first, I thought this was just me thinking of music and making melodies in my mind. I was a musician, so this was understandable. After a few moments, I realized that the music was no longer in my mind but had moved outside of my head and seemed to be playing in the room around me. It was very faint, but there. As I listened closely, I realized that it was a man's voice. He was singing. The singing gradually began to get louder. It sounded Middle Eastern, an ancient language that I did not recognize. It continued to get louder and louder. It sounded as if the man was standing in the middle of the room singing. I began to realize where the singing was coming from. It was pouring into the house through the ventilation system. It seemed to be coming through all of the vents. I thought, "I can't tell anyone about this." I figured I had lost my last marble, that I was experiencing the aftereffects of all the gasoline that I had huffed.

As the singing continued, I rose from the couch and began to tiptoe out the room. At the time, we had a guest who was staying with us. As I worked my way down the hall towards his room, he flung the door open and said, "Do you hear that?!" My first thought was, "I'm not crazy." It wasn't in my head. What I was hearing was real. Events like this will get you searching and asking questions. The enemy will use these situations to try to lead you astray. God will use them to lead you to the truth.

These supernatural occurrences only became more and more frequent in my life. On one occasion, a few years later, I remember driving through town as the streetlights went out above me. There was a stretch of road that would go on for several miles. It was about two in the morning, and no one else was on the road. As I drove that stretch, every streetlight above me would go out as I passed under it. This strange occurrence took place for miles as I drove. If that wasn't enough, I had an eerie feeling that someone was following me. The abnormal became my normal.

Two significant things happened in my life once I turned fifteen. The first was that I started playing in my first local bar band, and the second was that I started teaching guitar at Ricks Musik! It was amazing to have a job doing what I loved and to be working at the music store that I so often frequented. I still couldn't drive; my mother had to drive me back and forth to work. I had amazingly supportive parents, and they still are! One cool thing about working at Ricks was that I was around musical gear and other musicians all day. This was hard to beat. To this day, the guys I worked with at Ricks Musik are among some of the best musicians that I know. One of the guys went on to win some major blues awards. I had a good number of students, and I taught a wide array of music. I taught everything from punk to metal. I enjoyed teaching music theory as well. I wanted people to understand the mechanics of how it all worked. I was genuinely happy doing what I had always wanted to do. I was playing music for a living. Sometimes, I'd even come into Ricks wearing pleather pants, looking like a straight-up rock star. I loved the atmosphere. Ted taught there from time to time as well. I was now a full-time guitar instructor, and I was about to become a full-time performer.

My mother worked with a guy who happened to be a bass player. He had a band, but they had never played out. They would meet in a local basement to rehearse. He had heard that I could play and kept trying to convince my mother to let me join their band because they needed a lead guitarist. None of us were sure how this would work out considering I was only fifteen, and they wanted to play out. Being fifteen and playing the bar scene wasn't likely, but then again, neither was much that happened in my life. The band didn't seem to see my age as a problem. They had heard that I could play, and they wanted me on their team. By that time, I had created quite a reputation for myself. I finally made it over there for an audition.

It turned out the band's rehearsal spot was right around the corner from my dad's house. I made sure I got a smoke in before my audition. I showed up with a blue Washburn guitar and Crate amplifier, and I remember exactly what I was wearing: a leather jacket, white and blue checkered shorts, and my blue Chuck Taylor shoes. I was pumped. I loved having an audience. Once I was in and set up,

I didn't waste any time. I plugged in, and I let it rip. As I began to shred, I could see the smiles light up on the faces around the room. The bass player made sure to take credit as the one who found me.

Getting to listen to them was awesome as well. They were really good. The drumming was excellent; the rhythm playing was solid, and the vocals were fantastic. His voice was perfect for the music that they were playing. One of the songs that they covered was "Hero" by the Foo Fighters. They had some originals I liked as well. This was important because if a band didn't have good original material, they weren't going to make it. Having good originals was key. The feelings between the guys and me were mutual; the gig was mine. Not to sound immodest, but any band I had ever tried out for instantly recruited me. This was the beginning of a beautiful relationship that would jumpstart my musical career. We ended up naming the band Bidtter Ecstasy.

It was around this time I had a dream, which ended up being extremely prophetic. In the dream, I had met Mick Mars from Mötley Crüe, who I would later work with. In the dream, I was walking to school, when suddenly, Mick from Mötley appeared and was walking alongside of me. I said to him, "You have to come to school with me, because no one will ever believe that we were together!" I wasn't even a fan at that time. I would later become a Crüe fan and see them on their Carnival of Sins tour. In the dream, once we walked into the school building, I was getting ready to shout, "Hey everyone! Look who's with me!" It was at that moment that I turned around and noticed that Mick was gone. When I turned back around to face the students in the hallway, all of the kids were gone. On top of that, I couldn't find any of my classrooms. I was completely disoriented. The combination to my locker wouldn't work either. This dream held much significance and was multi-dimensional. I didn't know this at the time, but about ten years later, while in Pop Evil, I would be at Mick's house in L.A. writing with him. We wrote the music to what became the hit single "Boss's Daughter" on our second album *War of Angels.*

Now that Bidtter had all its members in place, we were ready to get to work. But it wasn't long before our bass player would leave the band. It just hadn't ended up being his scene. I brought in a friend of mine to replace him. The band would get together frequently to rehearse. We began working on cover songs, which included songs by Creed, and "Kryptonite" by Three Doors Down. The irony again is not only that I would end up covering many songs by Three Doors Down but that I'd later tour with them. I remember going to see Three Doors Down in Grand Rapids, Michigan, and waiting outside of their bus after the show in hopes of meeting them which didn't happen. Theory of a Deadman was new on the scene, and they opened the show. They were a Canadian-based band. I would later end up touring with them as well. We ended up doing several tours with those guys. When I look back now, I believe I can see how God was working things out in my life before I was even serving Him. With Bidtter Ecstasy, our goal was to get enough covers under our belt so that we could start playing out. We were a baby band. It was just the beginning for Bidtter.

We heard that we had some competition in town. There was a band on the scene called Klorine. Some of the guys in Bidtter had friends who were talking about these interlopers. We heard they were really good, but as far as we were concerned, they had competition because we had already determined that we were going to be the next best thing around. One night after rehearsal, one of the guys said, "Hey, Klorine's got a show in town tonight; you guys wanna go check them out?" Everyone was in. The only problem was that I was a minor, and we didn't know how or if I could get in. When we got to the club, there was absolutely no way that bouncer was letting me as a fifteen-year-old in the door. (This was the rock club I ended up playing at that was attached to the night club.)

What the bouncer did do, was let me sit on a stool by the front door next to the stage where I was allowed to watch and listen to them for three songs. I didn't mind sitting there because I was directly next to the stage and had the best seat in the house. The guys all went in, and we decided we'd reconnect after a few songs. When the band took the stage, they opened the set with "What's This Life For?" by Creed. I was beyond blown away. They sounded amazing. Musically and vocally, the song sounded just like the original. I was most impressed with their front man. His vocals were phenomenal. Plus, the singer was all tatted up and had this cool rock star vibe about him. It only took me a few moments to realize that these guys were going to be big. They were the real deal, and their potential was endless. Each song they covered was played to perfection. While I was there, they also covered "Bawitdaba" by Kid Rock and "Centerfold" by the J. Geils Band. They were at another level. After they had finished playing their first cover, "What's This Life For?" it was quiet in there, and I was the only one who clapped. The singer, whose name I didn't know at the time, turned to me and said, "Hey, thanks man!" It felt good to be acknowledged. These guys were really good.

On the ride home, we were all quiet. Not only did we have some competition, but it turns out these guys were way better than us. You could almost feel the disappointment in the air. If we were going to be the next best thing, we were going to have to up our game. We would have to be better than they were, and they were really good. I saw them again a few years later at another club in town. They had changed their name as well as a few members. They had two new guitarists. The front man and the rhythm section were the same. They had changed their name from Klorine to Two Heded Chan, taken from Two Headed Chang, who was the oldest living oddity at that time. He could be found in *Guinness World Records*.

The band was good before, but they were even better with this new lineup. They opened up the show by playing "Break Stuff" by Limp Bizkit. After that, they went into an original that I'll never forget, which was titled "Forked Tongue." They were amazing to watch live. I got to hang with the singer and some of his friends for a little bit after the show. For me, it was like meeting rock stars. They were rock stars in my eyes. They became a rival band to us, but I never held anything against them. They were my favorite band around. It was the type of band that I desired to be in. They were a rude, heavy, raunchy rock band. Though Bidtter had a good thing going, I secretly wanted to be in Chan. That would have been a dream come true.

Once we started playing shows, we'd play many of the same clubs that Two Heded Chan was playing. We actually started covering some of the same songs that they covered. Not only did we cover the same songs, but we played them the same exact way. This really irritated them. Nevertheless, we started developing our own following. To me, it didn't matter whether there was one person in the crowd or a million; I gave it my all every time I took that stage. I loved performing live.

We started out with bookings at a few local bars playing weeknights. You had to work your way up to becoming a weekend band in town, which we did. One weekend we had off, I found out that Two Heded Chan had a gig close by, and I went to see them play. I was still only fifteen years old at this point and already playing the bar scene. Because the club knew me, they'd let me in to watch some of the other bands from time to time as long as I behaved myself. Of course, behaving myself was short-lived. I would eventually start sneaking drinks. At one point, I was getting plastered regularly but never with my family around. Remember, I wasn't even able to drive yet. My family supported me playing but never wanted me to get caught up in the lifestyle.

When Chan took the stage, I was stoked. They invited me to come on stage with them as they performed "Break Stuff." I had developed a decent relationship with them just from seeing them around. I longed to be in that band. The vocalist looked after me as if I was his baby brother. To this day, he is one of the best vocalists and front men I have ever heard.

While I was on stage, some drunk guy was right in front of us jumping up and down. He had a drink in both hands and kept spilling it on the guitarist's pedal board. This infuriated me. He then tried to get on the stage. Without thinking about it, I reacted and shoved him off. He fell to the ground and broke the glass cups he was holding cutting up both of his hands. He got back up to come after me, and I hit him with a one-two combo blasting him back off the stage again. Suddenly, I had become Holyfield! This guy was much bigger than I was. He was eye level with me while I was on the stage, and he was on the ground. This time, while he was on the ground, security came and scooped him up. It turns out he was friends with the guys in the band, and they were used to his drunken outbursts, but I didn't care who you were; you weren't going to mess with the band that I loved or me. Because I was only fifteen, security asked me to leave.

# TURKEY

I was sixteen when I fell in love. I had started dating a girl who was a little older than me. She was the first girl I had ever been with, an older woman at eighteen. We had hooked up one night, and the love bug bit me. I truly thought I was going to marry her. She lived the next town over from me, and I still wasn't able to drive. At times she would come and pick me up from school. Because she was of age, she could legally come out to the shows. She was never loyal to me, and the relationship was short-lived. I had high expectations. It's funny how you ignore the signs when you're "in love."

Bidtter Ecstasy grew. We played the local scene often, and our fan base began to flourish. I was a promotional machine. In order to grow, I would continuously promote our band. I was constantly working to build our fan base. I would even slip flyers into the lockers at school. Most of the kids weren't even eighteen and could never have gotten into those clubs anyway. Our principal stopped me in the hall once to ask me what I was slipping into the lockers. I told him I was promoting our upcoming shows. He just smiled at me and said, "You can't be doing this." As far as I was concerned, this is what school was for, to promote my musical projects and jumpstart my career. School wasn't about learning for me; it was about promoting. It was my avenue to advance Bidtter Ecstasy. I didn't hate going to school; I just didn't like waking up early to go. Plus, if I was going to be a rock star, which I was, then what did I need school for anyway?

There were quite a few girls around during the Bidtter days, but I never wanted a fling. I had always desired to be in a relationship. For the next few years, Bidtter would be my band. We would play gigs and record our hearts out. We ended up with some pretty decent recordings. Two of our more popular songs were called "Gone" and "The Girl Next Door." I would send some of our recordings to a national rock group I liked called Hair of the Dog who had a hit single called, "Cadillac Jack." This was me networking and trying to get us connected. To my surprise, the guitarist listened to the songs and wrote back to me. He had a hard time believing that I was only sixteen years old, so I guess I was pretty good for my age. I was trying to work any angle I could to get us into the music industry.

At this time, Wes Borland had just quit Limp Bizkit, and the band was holding auditions in search of a new guitar player. Ted and I drove to Detroit for the audition. We left early in the morning. We figured the place was going to be packed. There would be plenty of people who wanted this position, but we figured we had what it took. It was about a three-and-a-half-hour drive to get there. Our ride up was filled with talking about life, smokes, and good jams. By the time we arrived, the place was packed out. Matter of fact, it was so packed that we couldn't get a spot to audition. I think Ted was more disappointed than me. At least we had some good quality time together.

A good friend of mine from Turkey and I had just seen Limp Bizkit in concert earlier that year. His name was Eren. I'll never forget the previous summer when I met him in Turkey, where I would still visit my family from time to time. I would stay with my grand-parents when I went. That summer, I would meet a friend whose life would be drastically altered because of our encounter. I had brought a carton of Marlboro Reds to Turkey with me. I figured American cigarettes would be a big hit over there, and they were. I could pretty much buy cigarettes anywhere I wanted in Turkey. Most of the time, I was able to get away with drinking at the bar. I remember going into one bar to order a drink, but the bartender would not serve me because of my age. Since I was a minor, he just stared at me; he seemed surprised that I was even attempting to order a drink. Since he would not serve me, I got up and walked to the other end of the bar where one of the other bartenders served me without a hassle. All my life, I had just kind of done what I wanted.

Not only was I young, but I stood out. I roamed the Middle East with long hair, a leather jacket, a Pantera cap, a Pantera t-shirt, cargo pants, and red Chuck Taylor shoes. I didn't fit in, to say the least. One night I ended up in some dingy bar drinking beer with a complete stranger. The situations that God has kept me protected in are amazing. But that summer, I met Eren. It was nighttime, and I went down to the seaside to have a smoke. I was lying under a tree looking up at the sky. Had it not been for the lit cigarette, no one would have seen me.

As I was lying there smoking, a group of kids came walking by. They were a loud rowdy bunch. I knew that they were trouble, and I was hoping they would keep on walking. That didn't happen. One of them stopped, looked at me, and said, "What are you?" They all started laughing. He said, "No, seriously, what are you?" They couldn't tell my gender because it was so dark out, and I had long hair. They could only see my outline. I came out from under the tree, and I introduced myself. I said, "Hi, I'm Tony, from America." They started laughing because in Turkey, Tony (spelled with an i), is a dog's name. At first they weren't sure what to think. Neither did I; I thought I might actually get jumped. The kid who seemed to be the leader said to me, "Well Tony from America, you're my new friend. You stick with me, and you'll be alright." Then he took me to get some ice cream. Eren was only a year older than I was.

I loved spending time in Turkey. I had so many childhood memories there. Every time I was there, the memories would come flooding back to me. Eren and I became super close. He stayed in the village behind our condominiums. We started hanging out every day. That summer was filled with drinking and friends. Matter of fact, the drink vodka and lemonade had become my other best friend. One particular night when I was at a local bar drinking, a bartender was working who happened to know my mother; he called her to let her know that her little boy was drinking vodka. I didn't know he made that call. A little while later, my mom walked in the door. I quickly pushed the drink away from me as if it wasn't mine. She asked me, "Were you drinking vodka?" I thought hard about how I would respond to her question. Finally, I said, "Yes." She said, "I know; they called and told me. I was just seeing if you were going to be honest with me." Usually when I thought I could get away with something, I wasn't.

Eren and I had become best friends. We were inseparable that summer. We did everything together. I didn't like being alone anyway, so I was happy to have a friend. One day Eren showed up at my door and said, "Come on, I want to take you to Istanbul." We didn't even tell anyone that we were leaving. Eren and I caught a ferry and headed out to the big city. It would be an adventure to say the least.

I didn't want my family to tell me I couldn't go, so I waited until I got there to tell them that I had gone. The first thing that Eren did was take me to a local hookah shop. I loved to smoke. We ordered apple-flavored tobacco. The green apple was my favorite. We were surrounded by Islamic men who were smoking and staring us down. We were kids, and neither one of us fit into that scene. Regardless, trouble seemed to be in our nature.

After the hookah shop, we caught a train out of the city. We didn't purchase tickets and decided to car hop. Eren proceeded to tell me how he did this often. As the ticket collector would near our car, we would go to the next car back. We kept doing this until we came to our stop. We just hoped we wouldn't get caught. Eren told me about a friend of his who had lost his head on the train that year. By "lost his head," I mean *literally*. He had stuck his head out the window not realizing that the train was entering a tunnel, and the wall clipped him taking his head completely off.

One of the days when we were in the city, Eren put a thick wooden stick up his sleeve and said, "Come on, follow me." We walked over to this guy who was getting into his car, and Eren confronted him, "Why are you looking at me like that, friend?" The guy said, "I'm sorry sir, I don't know what you are talking about." At the time, this gentleman was spinning his keys in his right hand, probably out of nervousness. Keep in mind, the guy had done nothing wrong; we were simply looking for trouble.

Eren, being streetwise, realized that this guy was right-handed. He grabbed his right wrist and asked, "Why are you acting like you've done nothing wrong?" Then he proceeded to beat him with the stick he had up his sleeve. As the guy cried for help, we took off. We looked back to see a group of men coming after us. We began to run. We jumped over fences and ran from yard to yard throughout the city. It felt like something out of a movie. If these guys caught us, they were going to kill us. Finally, we came upon a busy intersection. That's when I noticed a couple of the guys we had seen on the corner. They spotted us just as we jumped into a cab and took off. Trouble seemed to be what we did best.

We would spend that week hanging out in the city. We would go to Taksim and enjoy the metal clubs there. There were strips of cross-dressing prostitutes selling their bodies. This deeply grieved me. We even went to one district where prostitution was legal. We couldn't actually get into the gated city because of our age but only look at it from the outside. Though it was gated off, you could see the women in the windows flaunting themselves in front of the men as they passed by. Later, we would spend time with Eren's good friend whose father was a well-known *mafioso* in that area. We had an adventure, to say the least.

The following summer, Eren and his family came to visit us in America. It was amazing. Eren had gotten to show me around Turkey, and now I had the opportunity to show him around America, at least around my neck of the woods. I wondered what kind of trouble we could get into here! After a few weeks, his family went back to Turkey, but everyone agreed that he should stay in America for a while. He ended up staying with us for the next year and going to school with me. This was a bold move for him, considering he couldn't even speak English other than a couple of words. His parents figured he'd have a better future by doing his schooling in America, considering he kind of messed things up with the school system back in Turkey. The decision was difficult, but he decided to stay.

It took Eren a little bit to adjust, but he did. We shared a room together and went to school together. We were both in the German club as well. I'll never forget the day a girl in class bought him a Turkish Bible. It was evident that the hand of God was reaching out to him. On one occasion, Eren and I were supposed to go with the German club to Chicago, but I ended up sleeping in. As I slept, I had a dream of the guys in Korn. Eren ended up meeting them at the Chicago mall. Prophetic dreams were normal for me. I had a dream of meeting Kid Rock and having Christmas at his house once as well. I would later not only meet Kid Rock but spend some time with him and perform on his cruise, "Chillin' the Most."

Eren was a smart kid, so he easily picked up English, and he did well in his classes. He had some cool smoke tricks he could do, like blow smoke rings out of his nose, or blow a ring through a ring. He could also finish a cigarette in what seemed like ten seconds. This came from smoking in school bathrooms in Turkey. You had to smoke quickly so that you didn't get caught. Through a series of events, Eren moved back to Turkey at the end of that year. Later on, he ended up moving to New York, working his way through college, and becoming an engineer. Today he is an engineer in Istanbul and works on helicopters. Eren would forever be an integral part of my life.

Childhood

Practicing my martial arts

The Manson days

High school

Rocking out on my Washburn

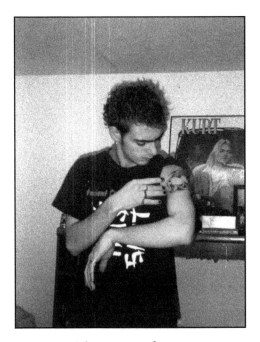

Admiring my first tattoo

On stage during my Two Heded Chan days

Rocking hard in Pop Evil

On stage in Pop Evil — Living my life 100 in a 55

Me onstage in Pop Evil with my Razorback Slime

On stage with Pop Evil at the peak of my career, five singles deep

# TWO HEDED CHAN

There was some serious division taking place in Bidtter. Some of the guys wanted the band to have a harder sound while others wanted to continue on the light rock path we were on. Our other guitarist started to sing some heavier tunes to give our vocalist a break, and unfortunately, that's where the division began. Aside from playing in Bidtter, I was still working at Rick's teaching guitar as well.

A cousin of mine was always trying to get us to play a house party for him. He wouldn't leave me alone about it. Matter of fact, he bothered me so much that I began to avoid him. He loved our band, and he particularly loved me. He wanted to host a rock concert at his house. It seemed like no matter how hard I tried to avoid him, I could not get away from him. One day at the grocery store, I spotted my cousin at the end of one of the aisles. I quickly left that spot hoping he wouldn't see me. Eventually, I ended up running into him, and there was no escaping it. "Hey man, I've been trying to call you," he said to me. I was aware. I realized there was no getting out of it. I finally agreed to play his party. The band was extremely excited about it. The party would be held at my cousin's house out in Greve Land.

On the day of the show, we showed up with a sound guy and a full sound system. We set up in his garage. When the party started, it started loud. We rocked it. We opened up our first set by playing covers such as "Hemorrhage" by Fuel, "One Step Closer" by Linkin Park, and "Attention Please," by Caroline's Spine. We played a lot of our own original stuff as well. It was around eleven at night when the police showed up. My cousin had a history with the police and was not in his right frame of mind at this time. I watched as he bolted through the garage, out the back door, and off into the night. The cops were pleasant; they simply asked us to turn it down due to a noise complaint. That was pretty much the end of the party. With the party coming to a halt, I walked down to the lake to get a smoke in. As I was smoking, I heard some noise in the canoe that was ashore by the lake. I walked over there to see what was going on. It was my cousin. He was hiding out. He asked if the police were gone and whether it was safe to come out.

While Bidtter Ecstasy continued to play shows, I would go and watch Two Heded Chan any chance I could get. They were my favorite band to go and see live. They would usually invite me to play on stage with them as a guest. What I didn't realize at the time was that they were looking for a lead guitar player since their other guitarist had quit. I was being auditioned without realizing it. They ended up inviting me to a few of their rehearsals. Finally, they said to me, "If you want the position, it's yours." Bidtter had already started falling apart, and there was no way I was going to pass up playing with my dream band. At eighteen years old, I had just graduated from high school when I became the new official lead guitarist for Two Heded Chan.

I already had the gear. At the time, I was playing through a Mesa Boogie Triple Rectifier. This thing was built for stadiums. If you turned it up to one, it would rattle the walls of the house. All of the greats were playing Mesa at this time. This was an interesting time for me because everything was changing. I was going through many transitions. Joining Chan and graduating from high school were major mile markers in my life. I knew I was in the right band. This was the band that could make it. I was sure that we were going to rock nations. We had all of the right elements needed to get the job done.

At this point, most of Chan's following had dwindled. We were basically starting over from scratch. Though much of their crowd was gone due to member changes, their potential wasn't. It wouldn't be long before we would rebuild a following and a team. We had some diehard fans who would follow us everywhere we went. Eventually, some of them would become our road crew, and one of them, our manager. When we started traveling and playing shows, we had built up such a following that anywhere from one hundred to one hundred and fifty people would travel to catch our shows, regardless of the distance. Our fans would find out what hotel we were staying in, and they would get reservations there as well. It became one big party. Bathtubs were turned into ice chests for beer and other types of liquor. We had such a diehard following that our fans were starting to get our logo tattooed on their bodies. We began to take off, and we took off quickly. We were quickly developing what I would call "The Chan Army." Since I had just turned eighteen, I had gone and gotten my first tattoo as well. From the time I could get tats, I knew that I wanted sleeves (where tattoos cover most or all of one's arms). I loved the tattoo culture.

Chan was pretty much playing the same bars as Bidtter Ecstasy. We all played the same circuit. We did both covers and originals. We were a much heavier band than Bidtter. We were like Three Days Grace and Mudvayne all rolled into one. We sounded a lot like Five Finger Death Punch. We were definitely heavy. As far as covers were concerned, we covered a wide variety of music. We covered anything from Chevelle and Three Days Grace, to Staind, all the way to Poison. We could take you straight from head banging to an '80's ballad. Some of the titles of our originals were, "Bravery," "Everlasting," and "Forked Tongue." At the time I had started dating a girl on and off. We had gone to high school together though I never really got to know her at that time. She was away at college but would connect with me while she was in town. A lot like my cousin, her persistence was what pulled me in. Once in a while, I would drive up to her school to see her. She didn't care for college and would soon drop out. The truth is, my heart wasn't in the relationship. I would consistently pursue other girls.

Now that I was in Chan, it had opened me up to the party lifestyle that I had been looking for. One night during a show, I got plastered out of my mind. I would generally take shot after shot. Somehow I had a way of holding myself together. People would think that I was alright, yet I would be completely wasted. I didn't care much for beer, but aside from that, I'd drink it if it was available. I enjoyed taking shots and drinking mixed drinks. I could out-drink, and keep up with, the best of them. But this particular night, I literally closed the bar down. I was having such a good time partying that I had failed to notice everyone had left. It was about 2:15 am when I looked around the room and said, "Where is everybody?" The waitress said, "Honey, it's after two. We're closed, and everybody is gone."

She offered me a ride back to her place and said that I could sleep on her couch. I probably should have taken her up on that offer. I don't know how I thought I was in any shape to drive. And considering the way that I was living at that time, it wasn't like me to pass up an opportunity to go home with a woman. But, I said, "Nah, I'll be good. I can make it home." Wherever the sober mark was, I was way over it. I was hammered.

I went out to my car and started it up. That's when I noticed that everything had started spinning. I thought to myself, "I must have drunk more than I thought." I decided to wait a while before I drove home. At some point in the process of waiting, I must have passed out. I remember waking up with my door wide open and me hanging out of it. My seatbelt was still on. It was eight in the morning. My car had been running all night and was now on empty. To my benefit, there was a gas station directly across the street. I got gas and headed home. My time in Chan was filled with many crazy nights, and we were just getting started.

It wasn't long before our bass player left because he wanted to get out of the bar scene, and we had to find a replacement. It seemed like I played in bands that had a history of bass players who quit. Our drummer's brother filled in for some shows, but eventually we ended up bringing in my bass player from Bidtter.

Chan played some rowdy shows. On one occasion we played a biker festival. Most of us camped out at the event. There were half-naked women walking around and contests I can't speak of. It was like something out of a Kid Rock video. We were a metal band that liked to party, and we attracted a party crowd.

Our manager at the time helped take us to the next level. Hawk was his name. Hawk and I would work tirelessly to get new gigs and to break into new territory. I would often stay the night at his house, where we would stay up all night smoking cigarettes and putting promotional packets together. We would ship these packets off to different clubs around the nation. The packet included our biography, itinerary, and music. We didn't get any bites at first. I'll never forget his famous saying though, "Stick with me kid, I can sell a Popsicle to a lady wearing white gloves." He was certainly very good at what he did; it was just going to take some time to break into these new venues. He was always bringing different friends to shows to check out the band. He could have single-handedly built our fan-base. It was time for expanding, and that's what we were doing.

Hawk ended up getting us booked at some of the best clubs in the state, even some of the best in the country. One club he got us into was called Ten Bells, in Grand Rapids, Michigan. It was a hard venue to get into, and rarely would they give a band their own show. It was the type of venue where you had to get on the bill with a group of other bands. Hawk was able to get us in playing a set or two. Some of those shows we would headline, and other times we would open for other acts. Hawk managed to get us a show at Ten Bells opening for the first time for a national act, Dry Kill Logic. Those guys were extremely heavy, so we fit the bill. We ended up playing several shows with them. We'd play with them a few times at Ten Bells and later on at a metal club in Flint, Michigan.

We had some diehard fans who would follow us around. Bob and Gene were two of my favorites. These guys were generally hammered when you saw them. If they weren't to begin with, they were by the end of the night. These guys came to a show of ours at Ten Bells and passed out before our set even started. Bob passed out at one of the tables, and Gene passed out in his car. This was not unusual for them.

Grand Rapids was a very hard scene to get into because Grand Rapids bands generally only rolled with other Grand Rapids bands. They only seemed to look out for their own, which made it a tough circle to break into. You had to pay your dues to get into the Grand Rapids scene. We were from Muskegon, and Grand Rapids bands tended to hate Muskegon bands. It was quite competitive. They had the attitude, "Can anything good come out of Muskegon?" Because Hawk could pitch us, we ended up on the bill with a lot of Grand Rapids bands although we were not accepted by them. That was the nature of the game. We didn't care either way. We knew that once we took the stage, we were blowing them out of the water, so to us it really didn't matter. Many of the Grand Rapids bands were decent, but they seemed to be missing the "it" factor. They were okay, but I didn't see many bands that had what it took to make it. You either had it, or you didn't.

We played Ten Bells quite regularly. One night, one of the crew and I ended up at one of the waitress's house. She seemed to be hitting on both of us, but I wasn't down with that. It was kind of a weird situation. She and I ended up making out in her bedroom, but she had left her bedroom door open and strategically turned the mirror so that someone looking in would see us. It was a weird scene, but weird is usually the type of situations we found ourselves in those days. Chad, who was with me that night, had recently found out that his girlfriend was cheating on him with a member of a band from Flint. It was just a messed up scene.

Choncho ended up becoming the drum tech for our band. Choncho was a friend of our drummer. He was always around partying and hanging out. Since he was there anyway, we figured we'd give him a job. Not only was he our drum tech, but he became our full-time roadie. His job was to load and unload the gear, set up the drums, and ensure that everything on stage was running smoothly. One thing about Choncho was that he always looked out for us. He was a big guy. I knew that he'd never let anything happen to me. One night a fight broke out at a club where we were playing. I don't know what it involved, but I know that Choncho got in the middle of it. His opponent had to be taken away by ambulance. Choncho felt terrible about it. He had the softest heart in the world, but he took care of business when it had to be taken care of.

The guys that surrounded us would have defended us to the death. On several occasions, we would have fights break out. On one of those occasions, I spit at a pro boxer. That probably wasn't a good idea. One of our fans came to my aid on that one. We had a lot of guys around us who could throw down with the best of them. One guy who used to hang out with one of our crew was named Sandy. Sandy was known for having an iron fist. During one of our shows, a friend of mine had got himself caught in a scuffle. I hadn't seen him in a long time. He simply wanted to come out to enjoy the night. I was rocking out stage left when I saw him getting caught up with some guys out of the corner of my eye. The fight got dragged outside. I was about to throw my guitar down and go to his aid when Sandy yelled, "I got it!" and took off out the door. The story has it that he squared up with the dude and in one hit, busted his nose wide open. He had lived up to his name, "The Iron Fist."

Years later, early on in Pop Evil, Sandy would have to throw me out of a club for trying to start a fight with one of the guys from Black Stone Cherry. I was little, but I had a fire on the inside of me.

My lead singer once said to me, "You're like a Chihuahua with the biggest bite I've ever seen." I had a short fuse. I seemed to snap at the drop of a hat for which I was dubbed "The Turkish Terror," and later, "The Turkish Tornado." I would go from being the life of the party to being the "Tornado." Something on the inside of me would just snap and change my whole demeanor.

We were the local openers for the show I got kicked out of. The line-up was Pop Evil, Black Stone Cherry as direct support, and Saliva as the main act. I, as usual, was drunk out of my mind. I went to shake one of the band members' of Black Stone Cherry's hand and say good job, but he just kind of stared at me. I instantly went into tornado mode and went off on him. I said if he wanted to go, to take his best shot. I had a studded belt on at the time, which I took off and was going to use as a weapon when Sandy, who was working security that night, came and scooped me up. He had me held up by the arms and was literally carrying me through the club to the exit. "Sandy, you better put me down, man," I said. "We go way back, bro. Is this how our relationship is going to end?" He said, "I'm sorry man. I don't want to do this, but I have to do this." He set me outside the door of the club and shut it on me.

I had just got kicked out of a show that I was playing in! I was so angry that I walked around outside of the building smacking it with my studded belt. Meanwhile, Josey Scott, from Saliva, was standing about thirty feet away signing autographs. He just looked at me as if to say, "What is this crazy guy doing?" Years later, when I toured with Black Stone Cherry, everything seemed good between the band member and me from that night. I thought he either forgot about it or didn't recall that it was me. When I brought it up, he said, "Oh I remember! It's water under the bridge." We both laughed about it.

Hawk continued to get us shows. Because we had a connection to playing with Dry Kill Logic in Grand Rapids, Hawk tried to get us on the bill with them in Flint. The band requested us. This was a venue that we had wanted to get into for a long time. It was a metal club called The Machine Shop. The Machine Shop featured some local stuff, but they primarily housed national acts. The owners said that they weren't going to just throw us on the bill but would have us out on a weeknight to see how we did. Potentially, if we did well, we could get on some of the shows there. In this business, it's all about bodies. Bodies equal sales. If you could pull a big enough crowd, you were in. Hawk was finally able to get us a midweek show at the Shop. About sixty of our fans followed us to that show on a weeknight. That was huge, and it spoke volumes about our band. The club owners were extremely impressed. Because of our turnout, we were able to get on the bill with Dry Kill Logic. We ended up playing a few more shows with them.

We built quite a relationship with The Machine Shop, and we played there often. The next time we played there, we decided to stay the night. Hawk was so excited because he had gotten us a great deal at a motel right down the street from the club. He had gotten us rooms for $30.00 a night. Something seemed very off about this. Once we got to the motel, we realized why. We were staying at prostitute central. Hookers were hanging out in front of the entrance gate. The motel rooms only had one channel on the television sets, and it was set to pornography. One of the guys in our crew found a crack pipe under his mattress. Some of the fans that had followed us down had two big guys walk into the room and case the place. No one said anything when they came in. They didn't know if they were looking for drugs or if they were there to rob them. It was a tense situation. Then they turned around and walked out. Those fans immediately checked out of that motel. On the other hand, some of us decided to stay there, and I was one of them. I ended up hooking up with a girl at the Shop and bringing her back to my motel room for the night. Wasn't that classy? I brought her back to the motel that only played porn. Though Flint became like a second home to us, we never stayed at that motel again, which was probably a good idea.

We had just finished recording our debut album titled *Teratous Genes.* I was stressed most of the time during our studio sessions because I would write overly complicated parts to play. They sounded cool, but were extremely difficult to pull off, especially the guitar solos. *Teratous Genes* was a concept album. *Teratous genes* is a Latin term meaning any abnormality of structure or function present at birth including those that do not manifest until later in life, also known as birth defects. People with a birth defect may feel like outcasts from society. This album represented those who felt like they didn't fit in or belong. The album contained a lot of solid crunchy riffs. It was very straight forward. It had strong vocals as well as ripping guitar solos. "Where I Rest," and, "Operation One Night Stand," were two tracks off of that album.

Hawk was known for getting us into venues that otherwise seemed impossible to get into. He prided himself on this. He was always up for the challenge. He booked us at a venue completely new to us called "Planet Rock," in Battle Creek, Michigan. The owners were wonderful people. They were a sweet older couple. They loved us, and we adored them. Our first show there was with a band called Hayseed Dixie. Hayseed Dixie was a tribute band to AC/DC, only they were bluegrass. These guys were radical. They would take classic rock songs and perform them as bluegrass tunes. One of the guys in the band told us how his father had written "Dueling Banjos." We played with them on several occasions, honoring them by wearing overalls to one of the shows.

These guys were good ol' southern boys. We grew close to them. The night we met and played with them, we found out that they were staying at the same hotel that we were. That night was out of control. I remember one of our guys roaming the hall in a drunken state talking to himself about peanut butter and jelly sandwiches while one of the crew ran naked through the hallway. That night we decided to play drunken bowling. We took our empty beer bottles and set them up like bowling pins at the end of the hallway. We would either roll something towards them or go crashing into them ourselves. I don't know how we didn't get thrown out of some of those places.

Planet Rock in Battle Creek and the Machine Shop in Flint would become two venues where I would play at for years to come. The band was growing, and Hawk was doing a stellar job of beginning to book us with national acts. One of the bands that Hawk booked us with was a band called Dope. Dope was melodically heavy. They had so many songs that I liked. They were mainstream yet underground at the same time. I really liked that about them. These guys knew how to put on a show. They had a vibe that was White Zombie and Mötley Crüe all rolled into one. I was looking forward to playing with them but more so to seeing them live. I could not wait to see Dope live for the first time! I was hoping that they would be as radical in person as they were on their albums.

The show ended up being a flop. Apparently, it hadn't been promoted, and there were maybe thirty-five people there. That's not an under-estimation. The place was empty. I wondered if Dope would still play and how they would perform without a crowd. Sure enough, they came out and smashed it, but they only played three songs. They were one of the best live bands I had seen. After three songs, the vocalist, Edsel, shut it down since there was no one there and pulled his band off the stage. They all ended up drinking at the club's bar. I would have really liked to stay and connect with them, but we had to head back to Muskegon because some of the guys had to work in the morning.

We ended up playing with Dope a lot. On one occasion, we played with them in Detroit. You had to sell tickets to be on the bill. The venue was in an extremely shady area. The bouncer there told me how the week before someone had gotten shot dead in the street right outside of the club. We were told not to stray too far from the venue. There were a bunch of local bands on the bill earlier that day. We were the last local band to perform on the bill although we were no longer local but had become regional.

The bands that went on after us that evening were Twisted Method, Motograter, and Dope. Earlier that day, I walked outside while one of Dope's road crew was getting reamed out for not doing his job. That roadie and I would end up working together years later. That night our singer took the stage with Motograter performing a song with them; it turned out to be their last show. The singer from Motograter would go on to form the band Five Finger Death Punch. When Dope took the stage, it was mayhem in that place. Dope had dummies, replicas of themselves that dropped from the rafters. The dummies were hanging from nooses in orange jumpsuits representing jail outfits. They always put on a stellar show. That ended up being one of the last shows we played with Dope.

# ROSE

Two Heded Chan continued to blow up, and Hawk still managed to get us on the bill with many national acts. I decided that I would take some courses at a local community college and signed up for music and communications classes. One day while sitting on the grass in the courtyard between classes, I heard music playing. I knew live music when I heard it. It was coming from the school's cafeteria. It was a song I knew well. Whoever the band was, they were playing "Interstate Love Song" by Stone Temple Pilots, and they were doing a mighty fine job of it as well. I walked into the cafeteria and grabbed a seat. They followed that song up with "Alive" by Pearl Jam. The name of the band was Pop Evil. They were a local band from Grand Rapids, Michigan. I had heard of them before but never took enough interest to check them out. They weren't bad at all. In actuality, they were really good. After their set was finished, I walked over to talk to the guitar player. I let him know that I enjoyed his playing and that he did a great job. Little did I know that I was talking to my future bandmate, and little did he know that he was talking to his future lead guitarist. Chan ended up playing an outdoor festival alongside of them though I didn't have the opportunity to catch up with any of them that day.

I started dating a beautiful girl named Rose. Rose and I would date for the next several years. I first saw her at one of the clubs where we played. I would see her there from time to time. The first time I saw her, I was instantly attracted to her and wanted to get to know her. Eventually, she came out to one of the shows we played, and I was able to briefly chat with her. I invited her to a show we were playing in Grand Rapids, and she actually came out. That's when I got her phone number. To this day, her phone number is etched in my brain. I think I repeated it over and over again so just in case I lost it, I'd remember what it was. Rose and I began talking and building a relationship. I was adamant that she was mine. At one of our shows a fan was hitting on her. I made sure to check the brother and to let him know that she was taken.

Rose and I had a great time together, unless there was alcohol involved. If one of us was drunk, it seemed like all hell would break loose. On occasion, I remember playing shows and watching Rose walk in the door. She'd have that glazed-over look on her face which meant she was already plastered. You just knew what kind of night it was going to be. My heart would sink in my chest, and I'd just want to run away. I'd be devastated. It's not that I didn't drink; it just usually meant that the night was going to be a disaster. She'd be completely hammered, getting up on somebody while I was playing and could do nothing about it. On one occasion, she left the bar with another guy. We had quite the dysfunctional relationship, yet we loved each other. We both had our problems. Believe me, I was far from faithful myself, but I guess I had a double standard.

Despite the difficult times, Rose and I had a blast together. We enjoyed watching horror films together and listened to the same kind of music. In October, we would take weekend trips and go to Fright Fest at Six Flags. We loved theme parks, especially during the Halloween season. Upon entering the theme park, the entire pool was red as if the water was blood. We had a lot of fun, and we did a lot of fighting. Neither one of us had it together at the time. If we were fighting, there was generally alcohol involved and lots of it. One time, Rose and I came back to my dad's house after a night at the bar. We had been arguing a little bit. All of the lights were off in the house, and it was pitch black. As soon as we got into the house she attacked me, and we both ended up on the ground. When this occurred, my brother and his friends came out from hiding, and everybody ran to his room. They had planned to scare us, but they didn't plan on us fighting.

We had such a love-hate relationship. Yet, how could I expect her to trust me? Nothing about me or my life was trustworthy. I was always doing something crazy, and I'm sure that at times it was extremely embarrassing for her. If she wasn't out to see what I was up to, her friends probably were and reported it. For example, during one of our shows, I got the grand idea to trade clothes with a girl in the audience. There was heavy drinking involved, of course. I thought it was brilliant. I grabbed the girl, and we ran to the men's bathroom. The security guard actually guarded the door while we changed. No one was allowed to enter. I'm surprised I didn't make a move on her right there in the stall. We swapped clothes. She put on what I was wearing, and I put on her tight black tank top, pink mini skirt, and knee-high go-go boots. I came out of that bathroom and walked right to the stage for our last set.

I could be completely drunk yet function as though I was completely stable. I wouldn't slur my words or stumble around. It didn't even affect my playing. No matter how drunk I was, I could play with my eyes closed and not miss a beat. When I took the stage, we opened our set by playing "Loco" by Coal Chamber. There must have been a hundred people on the small dance floor of that bar. They went nuts. I was dangerously spontaneous like that. I would get a crazy idea and just go for it. No one ever knew what I was going to do. That wouldn't be the last time I wore women's clothing on stage.

The band was growing like crazy. We were starting to outgrow some of the venues that we were playing. We were a local band making a massive impact. There would be lines of people wrapped around the outside of the clubs we were playing at just waiting to get in and see us. Our fan base was epic. People would be at our shows through blood, sweat, and tears. We had diehard fans. As the band got bigger, so did our shows. Hawk was even able to get us on a show with Alter Bridge and Whitesnake. This would be the first of many times that I would meet Mark Tremonti, and the first of many shows that I would play with Whitesnake.

Chan ended up entering West Michigan's Heavy Weight Battle of the Bands. We knew we had what it took to win it; we just figured the whole thing was rigged. The chances of a Muskegon band winning a Grand Rapids Battle of the Bands was slim to none. To our surprise, we won the first round. Then we won the second round, and then we ended up making it to the finals. After the final performances, they announced the winner: "This year's winner of the Heavy Weight Battle of the Bands is, Two Heded Chan!" We, along with our fan base, went nuts. We had just won West Michigan's heavy weight championship.

Choncho picked me up, put me on his shoulders and started carrying me around. It was such a win and a celebratory moment for us. The prize was a little bit of cash, some free tattoo work, and what we were looking forward to the most, studio time. With such a big win under our belt, it was time to start recording our next album, *Audio Warfare*. You can still find some of the songs from that album on the Net today. A few of the tracks from that album were "Shut Up," "Olio," and "Everlasting." They were all great songs, but "Everlasting" and "Shut Up" really grooved.

I felt like I was living my life at 100 mph and burning the candle at both ends. The band was having great success, but my personal life was in shambles. Rose and I were falling apart. There were nights at the bar where Rose would literally attack and claw at me, and times where I would slam my drink down leaving her standing there by herself. Emotional and unstable, I was either up or down. I guess Rose and I both were. We were both spiraling out of control. I loved the party scene, and that didn't help any.

One night, Chan was hosting an up and coming national act that had just played in town. The guitar player came back to my house, and I gave him my room for the night. As an example of how out of control I was at this point, in a drunken stupor, I spontaneously barged in on the guitar player, who was with a girl, and pretty much suggested a *ménage a trois*. I couldn't seem to get it together. As much as I wanted to be faithful to Rose, it was so hard for me to do.

A kid had contacted me who wanted to job shadow me for a day. It was a school project where you go to work with someone who did a job you wanted so that you could see what it was like to really work in that field. He wanted to be a rock star, so he asked if he could job shadow me as a class assignment. The morning he showed up, I had forgotten he was coming over. I had slept in hours past the time we were supposed to meet. I didn't know that he had let himself into the house. I woke up and put a towel around my waist, escorting a blonde girl out of the house who had been with me the night before. It looked like a scene from *Two and a Half Men*. I looked at him and said, "Here we go!"

The reality was, we were becoming rock stars. We were becoming what I always believed we were. Hawk started getting us some shows with a national band called Mushroomhead. These guys were heavy and dark, and they seemed to like our band. One night after a show, the drummer invited me onto their tour bus to chat with him. I think they were scouting our band. He invited us to play with them for a show in their hometown of Cleveland, Ohio. This was a huge deal. Not only would we play for the show, but our huge fan base would follow us down there. Mushroomhead was a dark, dark band. Their song title, "Sun Doesn't Rise," somewhat captures how dark they were. Adding to the darkness was the name of one of their vocalists, *Jeffrey Nothing*. That whole scene was extremely dark and creepy.

Even being backstage in that setting creeped me out. But, we were breaking into an entirely new scene. Rose and I were still dating, and one night she invited me over to her house to spend time together. She and I were going to have a special night, just the two of us. The moment I walked into her house, there were two things that stood out to me. The first was that she was drunk, and the second was that she barely had any clothes on her body. She had a tight jacket on that barely covered her bottom, and that was it. I noticed an empty bottle of wine on the counter, and I thought to myself, "This is not good." We were supposed to start drinking together, but she had started the festivities without me. She was playing it off that she wasn't drunk, but I knew that glazed-over look. The truth was that she was completely smashed.

With no more alcohol in the house, we had to go out and get some. We headed to the store. She was insistent that I let her drive. I didn't want to cause any problems, so I did. She went over the curb as she pulled into the parking lot of the store. After she parked, she said, "Okay, I'm going to run in and get wine!" I told her, "You can't go in there dressed like that. You hardly have any clothes on!" She didn't care. She was going in. She got out of the vehicle, slammed the door, and took off into the store.

I was so embarrassed. There was no way I was riding back with her. She was in bad shape. I got out of the car and started walking. After she came back out, she drove up alongside of me as I was walking and said, "Get in." I refused. "You're drunk, and I'm not riding with you," I said. She was so aggravated that she flipped me off, slammed on the gas, and then took off. Thank God, no one else was on the road. I watched as she sped away. Fear enveloped me, and I knew that I needed to get away from her. A few moments later, she was headed back in my direction. She was doing what seemed like 100 mph in a 35 mph zone. I hid in a bush because I didn't want her to find me. It happened to be midwinter, and I was walking back to her place to get my vehicle. I was utterly terrified of her in this state. I didn't know if she'd be kind to me or try to run me over. Had she gotten pulled over, she would have gone straight to jail.

When I finally made it back to her house, she was sitting in her car in the driveway. I got in the passenger side of the car and I said, "Rose, can we talk about this." She said, "I don't want to." She was drunk and fuming. Suddenly, she began to shift her car into drive. I quickly jumped out of the vehicle. Her house was back to back with another house with only a small yard to divide them. She took off and began driving through the yard and drove straight into a snowbank behind her neighbor's house. She was furiously stepping on the gas to get out, but she was hopelessly stuck. Rose had gone mad. Her dad would have to come to bail her out of this one; I was out of there. Rose and I dated a little bit after that, but not for long.

# POP EVIL

S trange experiences continued to take place in my life. One night after a show, a friend of mine from Texas and I were hanging out at my house and having a drink. We were laughing and having a great time as we talked about the past. As we were talking, we both simultaneously turned and looked at the doorway leading to the stairwell. On one side of the stairwell were a set of stairs leading to the garage, and on the other side a set of stairs leading to the basement. As we stared at the doorway, a creature walked from one side of the stairwell to the other. It was the size of an armadillo. It looked like something between an armadillo and a giant rat. Once in front of the doorway, it turned and looked at us, grinning through its razor-sharp teeth, and then proceeded to walk down the stairwell into the basement. We both looked at each other as if to say, "Did you see that?" We then proceeded to shrug it off and kept on drinking as if nothing had happened at all. These demons loved to make themselves known in my life though I did not know what they were. These odd and to say the least unusual experiences were my normal. Everything in my life seemed so surreal to me.

Chan was taking off, and as a band it was time to make some decisions. Dope offered for us to buy onto one of their tours, and if we were going to go to the next level, we were going to have to take some decisive steps. The next step for us as a band was touring. This divided us. Some of us were ready to hit the road while other members weren't ready to take that risk. It would have meant giving up job security to fulfill our dreams. Some of the members weren't willing to do that. This brought us to a crossroads. I wasn't ready to give up on my dream. We never ended up touring, and that's when I decided that it was the end of the road for me with Chan.

It was time for me to put another project together, which I could tour with because that was the ultimate goal for me. I was tired of depending on people, so I decided to go solo. I started playing acoustic shows by myself under the name "Anthony Emin." This way I could just go as I pleased. A buddy of mine was managing and funding me at the time. I played anywhere and everywhere, from pizza shops to health establishments. Wherever I could get a gig, I'd take it. All I wanted to do was play. I ended up booking and playing several shows at some of the venues I played with Chan and Bidtter. The beautiful thing about being a solo artist was that I could just throw my equipment in my car and go. I didn't have to rely on anyone else.

As much as I liked being a solo artist, I began to desire musicians who could back me. It was hard for me to stay out of a band. One evening, I ran into an old acquaintance at a store. He told me that his roommate was a bass player and looking for a band. I decided to give him a call. Matt was his name. Matt and I hit it off right away. He didn't mind playing bass in my solo project. Matt and I started getting together, jamming and writing frequently. The two of us realized we needed a drummer. Here I was building up what I had just gotten out of – a band. We found ourselves a drummer, and it wasn't long before the three of us were playing shows. It was no longer Anthony Emin, but we became Anthony Emin and the Music Box. We ended up playing one show in a high school auditorium. We found a bunch of props backstage, so we came out wearing some of them. Matt and I were also getting ready to start a metal project. We were just starting on the early phases of it when I received a phone call that would change my life.

I was lying in bed one night when the phone rang. I looked down at the caller ID and noticed that it was a good friend of mine. He didn't call often, so I figured he was just drunk and calling to mess with me since it was so late. I laid my head back down on the pillow only to hear my phone go off a second time. It was him again. Thinking it might be an emergency, I decided I better take the call.

"Hello?" I said. "Don't be mad at me bro," he replied as the phone seemed to be taken out of his hand. "Yo, what up," said a voice on the other end of the phone. "This is Leigh Kakaty, lead singer of Pop Evil." He asked what I had been up to and told me they were looking for a new lead guitarist. It turns out that my friend was friends with him and bragged on me up and down. We set up a meeting to talk. I met Leigh and his assistant at a Mexican Restaurant in Grand Rapids. We didn't waste any time getting into it. They were looking for a lead guitarist who could do some studio work for them and possibly fill in for some live shows. At the time, they were working with one of Kid Rock's producers, Al Sutton, in Detroit, and our local rock station was pushing one of their songs. The stuff they were doing was unheard of for a local band. They were a local band with a major mindset.

Though I wasn't excited about being a behind the scenes guy, I did like what they were doing and agreed to the position. Since I would be required to be at rehearsals and do studio work with them, I had to bail on the Anthony Emin project and the metal project that Matt and I had started. Matt was disappointed to say the least, but I was off on another venture. Pop Evil was beginning to build a name for themselves, and front man Leigh Kakaty was a genius. He knew how to market the band and keep the machine rolling. Pop Evil was his baby. Overnight I went from playing acoustic shows in pizza shops to working with Pop Evil.

Their hit single, "Somebody Like You," was starting to get some massive radio play. Those in the music industry and on the music scene know that local bands don't get played. It's borderline impossible. But these guys thought like businessmen not like a local band. They would dump the profit back into the machine, which funded its growth. Al Sutton recorded and produced "Somebody Like you," along with three other songs on an EP. The band then hired a professional director and shot a music video for the song. The radio station was so impressed with what the band was doing that they decided to give them a shot by putting them on the evening rotation. That's when "Somebody Like You" really started taking off and gaining national attention for Pop Evil. I had just partnered with a band that was getting national radio play. Could this be happening? It was. Not only was the single taking off, but after one rehearsal with them, Dave, their guitarist looked over at me and asked, "Want a job?"

I still wasn't an official member of the band, but things seemed to be pushing in that direction. Pop Evil was getting ready for a big hometown show, and I was to be a part of it. I was so stoked. It was at a club in Grand Rapids called the Orbit Room, which is no longer there. It was a great concert venue. I had seen Seven Dust, Drowning Pool, Three Doors Down, and many other great bands play there. I would now set foot on that same stage. I would play on the stage where so many greats who had come before me had played.

Excitement was in the air. It was cool to see people lined up at the gate to see the band. There was no opening band that night; it was just us. It was go time. The lights went down, and it was time to take the stage. We opened up with a track called, "Ready or Not," and we came out with guns blazing. For my part, I was energetic and entertaining, doing stuff like spitting water straight up, spraying it into the air. The band let me sign autographs with them that night. I felt like a star. I was a star! Something else significant happened that night. Right after the show, the bass player quit. Leigh was furious. After the show, walking out to the vehicle, I said, "Don't worry, I know a couple of guys. One of them has long black hair and fangs." He looked at me and said, "What do you mean fangs?"

Pop Evil would end up making two of the best moves they ever made. The first was that they realized Tony Greve wasn't a behind the scenes kind of guy, so they made me a full-time member. I was a front man with a guitar. And the second was the new bass player we brought in. We tried out a couple of different guys, but Matt was the one who got the position. This is the same Matt who played with me in "Anthony Emin and the Music Box." Leigh loved the fact that he had fangs. With Matt and I now in Pop Evil, the band had an entirely new dynamic. We brought a youthful vibrancy to the band and a metal edge. Meanwhile, "Somebody Like You" continued to shoot up the charts. Matter of fact, the song began to get so many requests that the radio station ended up moving it to daytime rotation.

Matt and I weren't from Grand Rapids, so we had to travel from out of town for rehearsals. It was as if the band became a new entity taking on an identity of its own. Pop Evil was finally morphing into what it was always meant to be. We began jamming and instantly writing a new song during one of our first rehearsals with our new line-up. That song would become our hit single, "Hero." We were in for the ride of a lifetime.

Pop Evil would travel and play shows on the weekends. This excited me. Sometimes we'd travel up to Traverse City, Michigan, and at other times as far down as Florida. I loved being on the road. I was still teaching guitar lessons throughout the week though it wouldn't be long before that would change. We all knew that we were close to something big. "Somebody Like You" just kept climbing the charts. We only had one station playing us, but it was a mega station, and its reach was massive. "Somebody Like you" climbed its way all the way up to number one. We were competing with bands like Metallica and Nickelback. Because of the publicity we were getting, these small venues where we were playing would be packed out. The way we would run it in those days was we would play a set of covers, then do our original set, and then close the night out with a set of covers. Some of the members didn't like playing covers since we had a song on the radio, but the truth was, that's what was paying our bills in those days.

One night, we were playing at a small club in West Michigan when I heard this massively loud crash behind me. We had just started our set. This was an all original show, and we opened up with "Hero" that night. I turned around to see what looked like a giant picture frame around my drummer's body and blood coming out of his head. We hadn't realized there was a glass case on the wall directly above his head. When we started playing, it rattled it off the wall and came crashing down shattering around him. Thankfully, there was only a little bit of blood because that could have killed him.

Due to my continuous travel back and forth to Grand Rapids for rehearsals, I ended up moving in with our manager and drummer renting an inexpensive room in a beautiful three-level house. The house was fully furnished and had a deck as well as a pool and hot tub. I had stopped teaching at music stores by this point and started giving lessons out of the house's basement – the "Pop House," as I had dubbed it. The house was essentially a bachelor pad. Many parties took place at that house. There was always a friend coming in to hang out or a girl leaving who'd been there overnight.

It didn't take me long to acclimate to Grand Rapids. I was already starting to make friends and meet girls. I fit right into the Pop Evil camp. We loved to be out and about. If we didn't have a show, you could usually find us at a local bar. The Anchor was one of our prime hangouts. One of our members frequented that bar so often that they let him run everything on a tab. He'd always come back in at a later date and take care of the bill. There were times we'd come back from traveling or doing radio interviews, and we'd go and hit that bar midday.

"Somebody Like You" had gone from evening rotation to daytime rotation to working its way up to a number one spot on the charts. Not only was "Somebody Like You" number one in our hometown, but we held that title for weeks. Our song had become the number one most requested song on the station. We were unstoppable. We were blowing up in one of the biggest markets for rock radio. Hometown heroes, we began drawing national attention. Labels began to question who our band was, why we were number one in Grand Rapids, and why we were only being played in Grand Rapids.

Despite the attention we were drawing, no one seemed to want to take a chance on Pop Evil. As many labels would look at us, just as many would pass on the offer to sign us. None of the labels were biting. Though no one was interested in signing Pop Evil, our booking price skyrocketed because of our number one single. It was obvious that the band was growing and making an impact. We knew it was only a matter of time. Our job was to hang in there and to continue doing what we were doing. It seemed like any minute we were going to go national. Journeys Shoe Store had even picked up our music video. They had it playing in every one of their stores across the country.

During this time, we were still traveling back and forth to Detroit for recording sessions. We were recording what would later become our first studio album, *Lipstick on the Mirror*. Getting to work with Al Sutton, who worked with Kid Rock, was pretty amazing. At the time, we were tightening up parts for the studio version of "Somebody Like You" and working on "100 in a 55." Since joining the band, I had come up with some additional guitar parts that we wanted to get on the tracks. We also began recording what would be released as our first single nationally, "Hero." This song was a heavy hitter.

As we worked on "Hero," a rep from Island Def Jam's Detroit branch stopped in to talk to Al. George, Jr. was his name, and he was an absolute metal head. He had heard Pop Evil before but wasn't interested in them, but the band had a different dynamic now and a brand new edge. The riff in "Hero" caught his attention. He wanted to hear more of the song. He was impressed. Matter of fact, he stepped out to make a call to his father, also named George, who had been a big-time radio consultant in the music industry. Everyone in the business knew who he was.

Our singer wanted to make a deal with Island Def Jam, but George Jr. didn't want to go that route. He wanted his dad involved in the deal. Our lead singer had called back to our local radio station in Grand Rapids to ask them if they'd ever heard of George Cappellini, Sr. The DJ, who also happened to be the head of the station said, "Have you ever heard of Tiger Woods? George Cappellini, Sr. is to rock radio what Tiger Woods is to golf." The Cappellinis were interested in working out a deal with us, but time would tell what that would look like.

# HERO

Leigh and I took a trip out to L.A. to work and make connections. NAMM, the National Association of Music Merchants, had an event there at the same time. You couldn't get in unless you were a vendor or with one of the vendors. A buddy of mine was the owner of a guitar polish company and had an extra pass to get me in. It was one of the wildest scenes I had ever seen. As I walked around looking at the different booths, I ran into guys like Joe Satriani, Wayne Static from Static-X, and Jason Todd of Shine Down. At one point, I found myself over by an exit when the doors suddenly blew open, and two security guards came rushing in demanding that everyone stand back. I remember thinking, "What is going on?" Suddenly, Nikki Sixx from Mötley Crüe walked in with a black suit on and a blonde on each arm.

Around every corner, I ran into a new star. That evening I found my way to a Dimebag Darrell tribute party right there in the Los Angeles Civic Center. Rita, his widow, was there hanging out in front of the entrance to the ballroom. It was surreal to me to be entering a tribute party to one of my greatest, but now deceased guitar heroes. The ballroom, lighting-wise, was very dark. As I walked through the crowd, I bumped into guys from Powerman 5000 as well as Bono. I watched many artists take the stage that night, playing Pantera songs in tribute to Dime. It was a treat to see Vinnie Paul from Pantera playing with Lemmy from Motörhead. During that trip, we also ended up backstage in the greenroom of the Jimmy Kimmel show. Uncle Frank from the show saw us standing in line and asked us about our Pop Evil hoodies. Once he found out we were a band, he said, "Oh you guys can't be out here!" He then proceeded to bring us back to the greenroom, which was entirely green. The L.A. trip was wild to say the least.

Once we got back to town, we continued playing shows. Leigh had set up a deal with Guitar Center, and we would play the Grand Opening of any Guitar Center in the Midwest. We would play under a tent in the parking lot while people waited to get in. One of the Grand Openings we played took place in Kentucky. There was a rep from the B.C. Rich guitar company in the crowd that day whose son loved our band. They took us out to lunch and then took us to the factory and gave us a tour. We left there with a catalog. They were willing to give us a non-exclusive endorsement. Matt and I agreed to it and were able to pick out a few of whatever guitars and basses we wanted. I was like a kid in a candy shop. I had picked out a couple of Mockingbirds. I loved those guitars. They each had their own feel. One of them really played great! It was perfect, just to my liking. Their only request was that we'd play the guitars live. That was no problem!

We continued to tour on. We traveled and played anywhere from Sault Saint Marie and Traverse City, Michigan to Panama City Beach in Florida. I loved being on the road, and I loved being a part of the party. Every night was filled with drunken mayhem. We were living the rock star life. But even amidst the success we were having, we couldn't get any labels to bite. One day we heard from the Georges who had scouted us in the studio, and they offered us a management deal. We had no other offers on the table, and the connections these guys had were insane.

We ended up taking the deal. They were determined to take this Grand Rapids band to the next level. George Sr. was responsible for breaking bands such as Guns N' Roses, Metallica, and Aerosmith to mainstream radio, and they were going to do the same thing with ours. These guys went right to work for us. Since we now had real management, our previous manager was repositioned. Each role was crucial. At the time, our management still hadn't seen us perform live. We had a show in Flint, Michigan that George Sr. flew in for. He was excited to meet and see the band perform for the first time.

Leigh and I had to go directly from the studio, where we were recording at the time, to the venue. Though I thought we played alright, George Sr. was completely unimpressed. I had a yellow Brazilian soccer jersey on that night, and I was playing my red Mockingbird. After the set, he looked directly at me and said, "Let me tell you something; don't ever let me catch you wearing a yellow shirt while playing that red guitar again, you look like ketchup and mustard." He pretty much reamed out our band, and he wasn't wrong. Dave was the only one he looked at and said, "This guy's got it together." He left saying, "We've got a lot of work to do boys," and we did.

There was a lot of work to be done, but the potential was unlimited. I was a little discouraged by George Sr., but he was right; if we were going to be a national act, there was a lot of work that had to be done. And we were willing to do whatever needed to be done to make it happen. But it was on. George Sr. and his son went right to work for us, getting us some national airplay. "Hero" would put us on the charts as a new up-and-coming active rock band. These guys were making fast and big moves for us. They got *Sons of Anarchy* to use "Hero" in one of their advertisements for their new series. In a matter of weeks, we went from being hometown heroes to having a single climbing the national charts. Not only did "Hero" climb the charts, it made it into the top twenty-five bracket, putting Pop Evil on the map. Not bad for some boys from Michigan.

Our management was working night and day to launch and jumpstart our band's career. They started getting us on several different stations regionally as well as on satellite radio. Wisconsin and Illinois were a couple of the first states to play Pop Evil. Once stations picked us up, we would then go and play those markets. It was a kick to hear the audience singing our song back to us. That meant that not only were we getting played in those markets but that there was now a demand being created for Pop Evil. We were starting to make an impact and beginning to develop a name for ourselves nationally.

With the band taking off, management and I both agreed on me switching from B.C. Rich to Dean Guitars. Though my deal with Dean wasn't exclusive, I made the decision to exclusively play Dean. I wanted to honor the company that was so graciously blessing and taking care of me. One of the first guitars I got from them was a Razorback Slime. Being a Pantera fan, I had wanted a Slime since I was a child, and now I was being handed one for free.

Right off the bat, Dean sent me several guitars of my choosing to play and would end up making me some amazing custom guitars. We toured hard, and we hit the markets where we were getting played the most. We spent a little time on the road with a band called

Veda. They weren't well known, and most of the shows were dead. One night, there were literally three people in the crowd. That's not an exaggeration. This was inside a massive building. We took the stage and played for those three people as if we were playing for five thousand. We may have been starting small, but we were headed to the top. With the management team we had and the radio play we were getting, we were unstoppable.

Because of some past beef with our management, Boston refused to play us. We were going to have to break into the East Coast on our own. We had a strong team that knew how to get stuff done. We had no major label backing us. Matter of fact, we had no label at all. George Sr. said to us one day, "We are going to do this thing grassroots style. We are going to build it from the ground up." That's exactly what we did. They would get us the airplay, and then we would go and perform the heck out of those markets. Our fan base around the country was steadily growing.

One day while I was at the Pop House, I got a call from management. "I got you guys on a tour," said George Sr. "You're going to be going out with a little band called Puddle of Mudd," he added. Because "Hero" was climbing the charts, the song gave us enough pull to land ourselves on a real tour. The tour consisted of us, Saving Abel, and Puddle of Mudd. Saving Abel was a relatively new band as well. They came onto the scene about a year prior to us and were blowing up. The tour would last three months, and we didn't know what would follow that. At the time, we didn't have a bus or any road crew. In fact, our tour manager talked his grandparents into letting us borrow their RV for the tour. We had to set up and tear down our own gear. I would like to take a moment to make a recommendation to the reader: Never let a rock band borrow your RV.

It was happening. I was getting ready to embark on the journey of a lifetime. I would finally be a part of a national tour. The tour was already in progress. We would be joining it in Pennsylvania. It was a sunny afternoon when we arrived at the venue. We pulled up right alongside the tour buses. Two girls were sitting in their car in the parking lot who kept looking over at us. They would wave and smile flirtatiously. I thought they were fans until I saw them get out of the car and walk onto one of the buses. I would see them at different shows around the country. The venue was beautiful, and the view was breathtaking. We were playing in what looked like a giant log cabin up in the hills of Pennsylvania. We meant business. Pop Evil had one agenda, and that was to dominate the stage every single night.

Before the show started, I was already walking around the venue trying to pick up girls. As the first act up, before we took the stage our tour manager gathered us together and said, "Guys, this is it! You made it. Go out there and crush it. Give it everything you have!" Not only did we give it everything we had, but we went five minutes over our set time. That just about got us kicked off the tour. This was day one. Since we didn't have a road crew, we had to pull our own gear from the stage when our set was finished. While we were tearing down, our tour manager was getting reamed out. Puddle's tour manager had made it clear that if we ever went over our set time again, we were off the tour, no questions asked. From that point on, we made sure we ended five minutes early. Tours ran on a tight schedule, and most tour managers ran a tight ship. They had to. We had a schedule to keep.

We hit it off with the Saving Abel guys. We would become very close with that band. Those guys had some serious major label support and the bus to prove it. They were just some good ol' boys from the South. We found ourselves hanging with their crew a lot. Life became one big party. A lot of the bands would come and party on our RV. That thing got wrecked. Every night would just be a drunken mess. One night a bunch of us were passing a bottle of Jack around when our singer said to one of the bands, "Why don't we go and party on your bus instead? You guys have the space, and it's way nicer." The response he got was, "No way, y'all are keeping it real over here!" The whiskey continued to flow. We fit right into the party. The other bands knew better than to destroy their million-dollar buses. By the end of this tour, the RV was trashed.

At one point along the tour, there was an incident with one of the bands; I just remember that their front lounge TV got smashed in. The RV became the "Party Bus." One of our guys took duct tape and created a Twister board on our RV's living room floor. We'd go from city to city smashing rock shows, and after the shows we usually ended up partying on the RV smashing drinks. This was a drinking tour. We threw it down. It was as if there was an unspoken motto that stated, "Drink or go home."

Most of the venues on this tour were at the House of Blues. We'd play different House of Blues venues around the country. Every night we were in a new state or a new city. Each show gave us the opportunity to prove ourselves as a band. We were road warriors. We were laying the foundation for what would establish Pop Evil for years to come. My dreams of becoming a rock star were manifesting before my very eyes. We were now accomplishing what so many deemed impossible. Playing at a House of Blues had been a dream of mine since I was a child. We took America by storm on this tour. Many nights we'd even end up on stage with Saving Abel. We played the House of Blues in Myrtle Beach, South Carolina, on Valentine's Day. We were directly across the street from an alligator farm which could be seen from our dressing room balcony. Several of our girl-friends, plus our buddy Dan, pooled together to come down for this show. Girls just came and went. Dan ended up meeting his future wife in Myrtle Beach on that trip, and they were married a year later. You're welcome, Dan!

After our set, you could usually find me at the bar doing Jager Bombs with the fans. I was a fan myself. Not only was I getting to play a rock show, but directly after our set, I was getting to attend one. By the end of the night, I was usually smashed. Most of us were. One night after one of the shows on that tour, my tour manager, one of the Saving Abel guys, and I all jumped into the back of a pickup truck to head downtown to a bar. Some fan wanted to take us out. It was supposed to be a short ride there. Once the pickup truck took off, he floored it. We were suddenly doing what felt like 85 mph in a 35 mph zone.. The driver seemed out of control.

Not only was this guy driving ridiculously fast, but he was fly-ing through every single red light. Out of panic, I grabbed my tour manager's arm and said, "Please, make him stop." I knew if we hit a curb, the truck would flip, and it would be over. Jed, our tour man-ager started pounding on the cab of the truck's window and yelling to the driver to slow down. The guy continued to floor it as if he didn't hear us. Jed said, "I'm gonna kill him." Once we finally pulled into the bar's parking lot, Jed pinned him up against the vehicle and let him have it. We were again spared by the hand of God.

As much fun as touring was, the road life wasn't always easy. You had to deal with a lot of different personalities. People were all deal-ing with different battles, struggles, and addictions. Yet all the bands

on that tour became like one big family. We all had each others'
backs. It's a miracle we survived that tour. The booze alone should
have killed us. We probably drank enough to satisfy an entire city.
We should have had tour shirts made that said, "I survived the tour."
Whatever you wanted, you could find it. There were drugs, there was
booze, and there were plenty of girls. Matter of fact, we had booze on
our rider, so the RV was always stocked up.

One night we had a fan bring us out cases of homemade moonshine. I had never had moonshine before. Everybody seemed afraid
to drink it. I thought, "We can't let a good thing go to waste" and
decided to try a little of it. It was amazing. It was blueberry moonshine. Matter of fact, you couldn't taste any alcohol in it. It was sweet
and tasted like blueberries. Within about ten minutes, I had already
drank half of the mason jar. My drummer looked at me and said,
"You drank all of that?!" I didn't see what the big deal was. Then he
realized that I had eaten the blueberries, which actually soaked up
all the alcohol. I figured, if you couldn't eat them, why put them in
there? I asked him why it was so bad. He kept laughing and saying,
"You're gonna find out."

The next thing I remember is my bass player laying me on the
couch to sleep and covering me with a blanket. I looked up to see
him taking off my boots. The entire room was spinning. I couldn't
even keep my head up. He said, "I'll see you in the morning," and I
was out. It was just another day on the road. The women seemed to
come and go as fast as the booze. I wanted to make the most of my
rock star experience.

In the midst of touring, we had to shoot a music video for
"Hero." We shot the video in the shop where our bass player used
to work. For an entire day, they shut the shop down and allowed us

to use their facility. It was dingy, grungy, and looked run down. It was the perfect place to shoot a rock video. We only had one day to shoot it. In the music video, the band was performing, and we each had our own individual fight scenes. The video's introduction even had a Mafia-like scene featuring one of our managers and our singer's brother who was our entertainment attorney. It was a fun video to shoot. This was the first music video I was ever a part of. We still had no funding from a label, and everything that we were doing we were doing on our own. The band and the management paid to have this video shot ourselves. Everything we were doing was getting done grass roots style, with no major label support. It was almost unheard of. Dean sent me a guitar specifically for this video. It was a Cemetery Gates Razorback. The artwork on it was beautiful.

# 100 IN A 55

As soon as we shot the "Hero" video, we got right back to touring without taking any time off. We ended up hitting the road with a band called Egypt Central for a short string of dates. The party continued on. One night we were all staying at a hotel with an indoor pool right in the center of the building. Our hotel rooms overlooked it. During a typical night of heavy drinking, one of the Central guys did a cannonball from the second floor into the deep end of the pool. When I say it's amazing that no one died, it should be understood that it truly is a miracle.

Most of the venues that we played on that tour were small clubs. We lived like hell and performed like it was our last night on earth. We were beginning to develop a road culture. We were always on tour. If and when we did have a break, it wasn't for very long. Even when I was home, I didn't want the party to end. On my breaks, I would continue to get smashed and hook up with girls. When one tour ended, we would just jump onto another tour. We never stopped. It seemed like we were on one long continuous tour that just never seemed to end.

After touring for "Hero", management decided it was time for us to release our next single. We released a single called "100 in a 55." The song took off, peaking at number eight on the charts. It was one thing to have a song in the Top 20, but we now had a single that was Top 10. As soon as it was released, "100 in a 55" rapidly began to climb the charts. If a song was doing that well, a band had to do a tour to support it: new single, more touring. "100 in a 55" was putting our album *Lipstick on the Mirror* on the map. We were gaining major recognition. So much so that we caught one label's attention. We ended up signing a deal with Universal Republic which re-released *Lipstick on the Mirror*.

With a label and two hit songs on the radio came bigger and better tours, oh, and a bus. We finally returned the RV to its original owners after we beat that thing to dust, and we upgraded to an actual tour bus. Having a bus was much more convenient because each member had their own bunk which meant private space. After the rise of "100 in a 55," we hit the road with a little Memphis band called Saliva. I had always wanted to see Saliva live, and now I was going to get to tour with them. Though our tour with Saliva wasn't long, it was certainly radical. One night we went out with them after a show in New Orleans. They had a camera crew and were filming for a potential reality TV show. We ended up being a part of a staged bar fight, but it was never released.

Tours seemed to go quickly. Everything had started blending together. I didn't know where one tour ended and the other started. Likewise, I didn't know where being drunk ended and being sober started. After the short tour with Saliva, we hit the road with Tesla. They were a great bunch of guys. The last night of the tour, we played at the Hampton Beach Casino Ballroom. It was Halloween, so some of the guys dressed up for the occasion. That night, Tesla invited us onstage with them to play "Free Bird" by Lynyrd Skynyrd. This wrapped up the show and the tour. It was epic. For Pop Evil, the tour continued on, and so did the party!

The bus we were traveling on during this time had previously accommodated Bret Michaels from Poison and Bob Dylan. One night, after an evening of drinking, I was standing in the hallway of the bus staring at the door to the back lounge. When I was drinking, it didn't take much to set me off. I had these super heavy boots on. In a drunken rage, I decided to run at and kick the door. I had only meant to kick it, but my foot went completely through it. I busted a hole in that thing.

Surprisingly, the owner of the bus wasn't mad. He was sad but not mad. He kept saying, "But it's mahogany." He didn't end up charging us for it. What can I say? It was rock and roll. I was no stranger to stupidity when I was drunk; however, of more concern was the fact that I often found myself bursting into fits of anger or rage. One moment I was the life of the party; the next, I was putting a bullet in it. Something would trigger me, and I would snap. Eventually, heavy drugs would balance that out.

Directly after the Tesla tour, we jumped on tour with a band called Framing Hanley. This lifestyle never stopped. During this time, we ended up cutting a publishing deal with Cherry Lane. But with "100 in a 55" doing so well, it was time to shoot a video for the single. We went out to L.A. to shoot it. The same director who directed "Hero", Jason Honeycutt, would now be directing "100 in a 55." In order to draw more attention to the band, we ended up getting a *Playboy* centerfold to star in the video. It couldn't hurt any.

In the video, she'd play the role of our lead singer's girlfriend. There was an entire breakup scene that went with it.

We filmed the video out in the middle of nowhere and shot some footage of us playing on the bed of a semi while the semi was moving! The only thing strapped down was our gear. We were cruising out in the desert flatlands. All I could think was, "If we hit a bump, I'm going to go flying." Miraculously, it turns out God hadn't created any divots in the desert. We drove for miles without hitting one single bump.

Knowing I could fly off the back of the semi at any moment was scary to say the least. At one point, I asked the director if we could strap me down. It was uncomfortable to say the least. He said we could but that it would look ridiculous for the video. I decided not to. Nonetheless, it was nerve-racking.

Dean custom made me a guitar specifically for this video. They sent me a Stealth. I had them turn the entire front of the guitar into a mirror to represent our album *Lipstick on the Mirror*. I loved using it live because the lights would reflect off it. I got good at targeting specific people in the audience and blinding them with my guitar. "Hero" got us in the door, but "100 in a 55" put us on the map as one of the hottest up and coming rock and roll bands. We were just getting started.

Our management got us on the Judas Priest tour. It was the 30th anniversary of their *British Steel* album. The lineup was us, Whitesnake, and Judas Priest. It was 2008. For me, this tour seemed to be a never ending Jager Bomb fest. It seemed like I was always drunk. One night, backstage at the AT&T Center in San Antonio, I saw Rob Halford down at the end of the hall entering his dressing room and shouted out to him. I had never met the guy. He had just entered his room but peeked back out to see what all of the shouting was about. In a drunken rampage I took off running down the hall after him having no idea what I was going to say to him. When I got to his door, I introduced myself and asked him about the tattoos on the side of his head. He must have thought I was a mess. I was.

On occasion, we would meet and hang out with the guys from Priest and Whitesnake. We had gone from playing clubs to playing 20,000 seat arenas. I was living my dream. We were playing to massive crowds and living the party life. One night, a band member and I got chased down by security because we stole and took off in one of the security golf carts. There may or may not have been heavy drinking involved.

When the tour hit Vegas, we were all excited because rumor had it that Vinnie Paul from Pantera might be coming out to see us. He had a house in Vegas and wasn't touring at that time. However, we were given strict orders by Whitesnake's management that Vinnie Paul was not allowed backstage. They knew that we were connected and had heard that he might be making an appearance. Apparently, one of the members from Whitesnake was still holding a grudge against him over some things that went down between them in the '80s. Whatever the reason, they did not want Vinnie there.

Here we were, playing Las Vegas. We were the first act up. I always loved seeing the stadium lights go down. There was such anticipation for a rock show. As we were playing that night, I saw Vinnie standing in one of the doorways in the back of the stadium. Since it was dark, all you could see was his silhouette in the doorway. That hair and cowboy hat were hard to miss. He had made it out for the show. Vinnie was also a huge Judas Priest fan. I was pumped because during one of my solos, I gave tribute to his brother Dime, by throwing in a guitar lick from a Pantera song. What better way to honor Vinnie's brother! What an epic moment this was going to be.

When it came time to play my solo, the band walked off, and I was center stage. I began to play, and my amp died. I had nothing. I walked over and kicked my pedal board. Everything just quit working. I took a bow and the crowd cheered, but I didn't get to pay tribute to Dime the way I had wanted to that night. Of course, once the band came back onstage and kicked into the next song, my gear started working again.

After our set we went back to the bus to meet Vinnie. He was there with his personal security. These guys were massive. They looked like they ate steroids for breakfast. They had no necks. They were super kind to us though. After a few minutes of hanging back by the buses, Vinnie asked Matt and me, "Where's your dressing room at? Let's go check it out." Matt and I looked at each other and smiled. We knew trouble was brewing. We let Vinnie and his security team lead the way, and we followed. The arena security had been warned not to let Vinnie Paul backstage.

I felt like we were living out a Pantera home video. It was amazing. I certainly wasn't going to stop him. Once we approached the back door, the arena's security guard said in a shaky voice, "Sir, I need to see your pass." One of Vinnie's giants literally picked the guy up, set him off to the side and said in a deep voice, "Vinnie Paul is our pass."

We proceeded to walk backstage and head to our dressing room. At this point, security was scurrying around backstage. After a few minutes, Vinnie said, "Eh, I don't want to cause any trouble," so we all got out of there. Our tour manager got reamed out by Whitesnake's tour manager for that incident, and of course, Jed ripped into us. We were like a couple of kids snickering during a lecture after just getting caught stealing cookies from the cookie jar. I'm surprised our tour manager had any hair left after dealing with us. We kept him on his toes! About halfway through the tour, Whitesnake dropped off the bill because their founder and vocalist, David Coverdale, had blown his voice out. We became direct support for Priest. We finished that tour having a bigger reputation than ever. Somewhere along the tour, my guitar tech lost my custom mirror Stealth. He claimed it had gotten left behind at one of the venues.

After the Priest tour, we just kept on rolling. In the summertime, we did a lot of festivals. Festivals were usually a reunion for us because we'd be on a bill with a bunch of new bands, but we'd also run into old friends like Saving Abel and Egypt Central. We played a festival in West Virginia called X-Fest. Avenged Sevenfold was headlining that night. This was prior to the passing of their drummer, Jimmy Sullivan, A.K.A., the Rev. We played midday. It was so hot, and I couldn't take the heat. I felt like I was going to pass out. I became nauseous during our set. The fact that I was drinking didn't help. It would be a rare thing to see me without a drink in my hand.

During one of my guitar solos, our other guitarist, Dave, and I would always meet center stage to rock it together. Well, he walked out there, but I was nowhere to be found. The amazing thing was that he could still hear me playing. I had walked to the back of the stage and was vomiting over the rail. Incredibly, I never missed a note. The summer festivals were amazing because you never knew who you were going to meet. At one event, I woke up from a nap to find Pauly Shore and Big from "Rob and Big" hanging out on our bus. From meeting Guns N' Roses members to partying every night, my life seemed like it had become one big circus.

# PILLS, BOOZE, NOW IT'S A PARTY

Drinking and drugging had become my life. I was always looking for trouble. We just hit the road with Buckcherry. I knew the Buckcherry tour was going to be complete chaos, and I couldn't have been more excited about it. They attracted a party crowd. That meant there would be lots of drugs, and there would be lots of women. Both were my forte. That tour was a party indeed. We were getting ready to play a show in Allentown, Pennsylvania. Our tour manager told us, "Guys, no parties on the bus tonight. I want to get some rest; I mean it." We all said "Sure," but in my mind I was thinking, "Like that's going to happen." We played the show and rocked it as usual. I liked Buckcherry. After our set, I would grab a drink from the bus then head back to the venue to watch them.

At the very end of the night, most people had moved to the front bar of the venue, but I got caught up over by the stage signing autographs. Security had come over to tell us we had to move it to the front room. It was almost closing time; I loved starting a party, but I hated seeing it end. I never wanted it to end; I hated being alone. Instead of moving to the front bar as security had mandated, I got this brilliant idea to bring about fifty fans back to the tour bus to party. I said, "Who wants to hang out and party? You guys wanna see the bus?" They freaked out. Our tour manager was about to freak out, too. I went from signing autographs for fans to inviting everyone onto our tour bus. It was rock and roll, right? Our manager wasn't around at the time because he had to square up for the evening.

I must have brought fifty plus people onto the bus that night. We busted out the drinks and cranked up the music. Our tour manager walked onto the bus to see it packed out. There were so many people that you couldn't walk through the center aisle. One guy crowd surfed. Because of the number of people jumping to the music, the bus actually began to bottom out hitting the pavement. All together, we would sing songs like "Sweet Caroline" and "Na na na na Hey Hey Hey Goodbye." I never wanted the party to end. I'm pretty sure our tour manager quit that night. I can't say how many times he quit, but he was usually back the next day.

At this point, I had gotten heavily into pills. I loved taking Adderall. It had the same effect as cocaine. I would take it right before I'd go on stage, then again around midnight when the party was just starting. I felt like I could take on the world. Another thing I loved about cocaine and Adderall was that I could drink twice as much as normal while on it, and I wouldn't get sloppy drunk. I met a girl who became my dealer on the road. The deal was that she would bring me Adderall if I would get her into the show for free. At other times this involved me getting her a backstage pass. She would bring me drugs, and I would get her on the guest list, plus one. I thought it was a phenomenal deal. It didn't cost me anything to do it, and I was getting free drugs out of the deal.

The drugs were free, the booze was free, and the women, well, the women came easily. I was bold when it came to women. One time, we were parked outside of a venue, when I spotted a girl waiting in line who appealed to me. It looked like she was with her boyfriend. When he stepped out of line to go to the bathroom, I ran off the bus and quickly invited her on board. When he came back, his girl was gone. "Trouble" was my middle name. But my use of pills and other drugs became more and more frequent; I didn't like to go without them. I had different connections in different cities. I wanted to make sure I always had a pocket full of pills, and hey, if I ran out, I could usually score something off of one of the other bands.

We were truly skyrocketing. It was now 2009, and we were getting ready to play one of the biggest events of our lives. We would be performing at Rock on the Range at Crew Stadium in Columbus, Ohio. Ironically enough, Mötley Crüe would be headlining it that year. (It was ironic because Crüe, who was headling the event, was playing at Crew stadium.) This was a three-day-long event. Bands playing the festival included Slipknot, Korn, Alice in Chains, Avenged Sevenfold, Shinedown, Buckcherry, Chevelle, The Used, Flyleaf, Rev Theory, and many more.

We were supposed to get booze from the venue, but someone had made a mistake on our rider, and we were left empty-handed. The best the venue could do was give us Capri Sun type tequila packets from one of the vendors. They gave us several boxes of them. Apparently, they weren't in high demand. No one in our crew wanted to touch them. I wasn't about to go without booze and took a packet of tequila with me as I wandered around the grounds of the venue that day. I remember the tequila being absolutely nasty. I was drinking while walking, gagging and trying not to vomit. Plus, the packets had been sitting in the sun and were warm. You know you've hit a new low when you're drinking warm tequila out of a packet.

We played the B stage that day. Our manager, George Jr., had come out to the event. It was our biggest event to date, and he wasn't going to miss it. He was so amped. He said, "Listen, if you can start a mosh pit and get this crowd jumping, I'll get you guys a Play Station for the back of the bus." Well, he was about to buy us a play station because from the first note we hit that place went nuts. We had that entire crowd jumping up and down. We had them in the palms of our hands. At one point during the set, an empty Jack Daniels bottle came flying towards the stage and flew right between Matt and me. We both gave each other a look as if to say, "That was close," and kept right on playing.

There was no end to the tour life or array of bands we would play with. Yet as the band got bigger, I found myself spiraling out of control. I found myself falling into a depression. Nothing I had made me happy or filled the void in my life. I had to stay drunk or high to be satisfied, and that satisfaction was only for the moment. There were days I was suicidal; I didn't know how to explain the pain that I was feeling on the inside. There was such emptiness; I was so empty that it hurt. Drinking or taking an upper was the only way I knew to try to stay happy. On the outside, my life looked successful, but I was screaming out for help on the inside. Part of why I liked to always have a girl around me was that I just didn't want to be alone. There were days when it wasn't about hooking up with anybody; I just wanted the company.

When we hit the road with Papa Roach, the party seemed to have gone to a whole other level. I loved watching Papa Roach perform. They were absolutely radical. One night I was hanging out with a Southern belle after our set; we were backstage watching Papa Roach, and I said to her, "Let's go to the bus and grab a drink, and we'll come right back out." Everything happened so fast. The ice chest on the bus was open as I was digging for drinks, and somehow it came smashing down on her finger. All I remember is her screaming out in pain and blood flying everywhere. She quickly wrapped her finger and took off for the hospital. It was bad. I don't know what ended up happening. You would think that might put an end to the night, but nothing was going to stop me from partying.

Drinking around the clock, and I do mean around the clock, became a lifestyle for me. The only reason I wouldn't have a drink in my hand was if there was nothing available or I was asleep. My routine was to drink, take a pill, then drink and take a pill. That was my daily routine. It was getting out of control. When I didn't have any pills to balance me out, I was a viciously mean drunk. I didn't care who I hurt. My philosophy was, I can always apologize tomorrow. Drinking became more than just for partying. I was so lonely; I would drink alone. At times it seemed like I hated myself and hated life itself. Darkness was engulfing me.

Late one night on the bus, I was in the back lounge drinking by myself. Everyone else was asleep. I was just sitting back there, alone, in that dimly lit room, chugging a bottle of Jack Daniels. I was at such a low place in my life. It was about 4:00 am. I picked up the phone and decided to reach out to a friend of mine. He awoke out of a dead sleep and answered the phone, "Hello? Hello, Tony, is that you? Are you there?" I was silent on the other end of the phone as I fought to hold back the tears. "I wanna go home," I said. He replied by asking me what I was talking about. "I don't want this anymore. I don't want this life anymore. I want off of this bus. I want to go home," I said. At that point, I threw my phone against the wall of the bus, smashing it. Then I passed out.

In my state of depression, I began searching. There just had to be more to life than this. It was so empty. I had everything I ever wanted, and it was leaving me high and dry. It didn't change me in any way for the better. One night in my hotel room, I opened the drawer of the nightstand next to the bed and saw that it contained a Gideon Bible. I decided to read it. I read the first verse, "In the beginning God created the heavens and the earth" (Genesis 1:1, NKJV). That was all I read. Reading that one verse brought me so much comfort. I wanted to keep that comfort, so I took the Bible with me.

The band had a few days off, and I decided to go home. I set the Bible on the nightstand next to my bed. I felt so much peace with it there. I felt as if it was protecting my room. I wanted to read more, but I didn't want to take it out of the room. I decided I would read more after the next tour.

We hit the road with Theory of a Deadman. When the tour ended, I was looking forward to coming home and reading my Bible, but when I got home, I noticed that the Bible was missing. This seemed so odd to me. Nothing else in my room or house had been touched. Everything was just as I left it except now the Bible was gone. I just couldn't figure it out. Something seemed strange about the whole situation. That night, I went to bed around midnight. As I was lying in bed, I suddenly felt a presence enter my room. The presence was so strong that I sat up in bed and began to look around the room. I decided to ask, "Did you take my Bible?"

When I asked that question, cologne, aftershave, and shaving cream bottles in the bathroom next to my room went flying off the counter and crashing into the wall. Suddenly, the presence of anger overtook my room. The spirit spoke. Though it wasn't audible, I heard it as if it was. It asked, "What is a Bible doing in my territory?" Why was it so angry about a Bible? What was in the Bible that it didn't want me to read, and why was its only issue with this one book? If anything, this sparked an even greater interest in me to read the Bible. There seemed to be a war going on over my life, and I was beginning to awaken to it. I was hanging in the balance of God reaching out to me and the devil attempting to keep me from grabbing hold of His hand. God continued to pursue me with everything that He had.

The band hit the road again, playing a show in Tennessee with a group called Boys Like Girls. It was a one-off for us, and it was an acoustic radio show that was held in a hotel ballroom. As we were backstage getting ready to play, a man came over and tapped me on the shoulder. He introduced himself to me and asked if he could talk to me after the show. His name was Pastor Jimmy. He said, "I'm going to be upfront with you. I'd like to talk to you about Jesus, is that okay?" Due to my interest in spirituality, I readily agreed. I told him I would meet him in the lobby of the hotel after the show.

We finished our set, and I headed off to meet Pastor Jimmy as I had promised him. I was double-fisting it as usual with an alcoholic beverage in each hand, which didn't seem to bother Pastor Jimmy. We hung out for about half an hour, just talking about life in general and what life on the road was like for me. Before we parted, Pastor Jimmy said, "Tony, what if I told you that Jesus died for your sins and was resurrected so that you could be with him forever, what would you say to that?" I said, "Well, let me think about it. I'll get back to you on that one."

Indeed, I did think about my conversation with Pastor Jimmy. I continued to stay in touch with him. I'd call him from the road, and we would talk from time to time. Sometimes it would be about God. Other times, he would check in on me to see how I was doing. He never seemed to judge or condemn me but only to be concerned for me, and rightfully so. With the sex, the booze, the cocaine, and the pills, it was a miracle that I was still alive. We continued touring, hitting the road again with Theory of a Deadman. I returned home from that tour to find a black bowler hat on my bed. I put it on, acknowledging that the demon had placed it there and thanking it for it. That hat would set my look for the next record.

# WAR OF ANGELS

We got out of our agreement with Universal and ended up signing with a label called eOne. It was time for us to begin recording our second album, *War of Angels*. The process of creating this album included Leigh and I going to L.A. to work on writing with some different artists. We wrote with Jack Blades from Night Ranger, and I ended up working with Mick Mars from Mötley Crüe. The song we wrote with Jack didn't end up making the album, but the song that Mick and I composed ended up becoming a single for the band, titled, "Boss's Daughter." Boss's Daughter was the third single we released from that album.

We recorded *War of Angels* in Chicago, the same time they were filming *Transformers: Revenge of the Fallen*. The album was produced by Johnny K, who had originally broken onto the scene with Disturbed. We would be in the studio for the next three months. We lived there. There were studios on each floor of the building, some of which had beds, a living room, a kitchen, and a full bath. For the next three months, my focus would be on hammering out this album.

We didn't waste any time getting to work. Johnny had us recording almost immediately. The first song we recorded was "Last Man Standing." The guitar and bass tone we got for that song would set the tone for the rest of the album. We just plugged in and went for it. We used a Fender Precision bass on it. It was so raunchy; it sounded like some old White Zombie stuff. We tried to see if we could get an even better sound than what we had, but we just couldn't beat it. The rhythm work on that album was recorded with a Les Paul. We used different amps to get different tones, depending on what it was that we were going for. Some of the lead work was done on a Les Paul and some on a Dean. Day and night, we would grind to work on this album. If it wasn't a band member's turn to record, there was a lot of downtime, but it seems like I was always in there, as I laid down all the guitar tracks for that album.

I had never worked with a producer like Johnny before. He knew what he was doing, and there was a lot of wisdom to be gained from him. I learned a ton of new studio tricks throughout this entire process. Johnny wanted to bring in a session player to play the acoustic parts, but I refused. Recording in the studio is much different than playing live. You have to be extremely precise. Johnny agreed to give me a shot, recording the acoustic parts before he would call anyone else in. I slayed it. Leigh and I also worked with multi-platinum songwriter Dave Bassett on some of these tracks.

Chicago was beautiful. I loved staying at the studio because at night you could look out the studio window and see the city of Chicago all lit up. Staying there was a delight. Aside from recording, we would take a break by going and playing a festival once in a while. One of those festivals was a fly-in date in Orlando. Sevendust was headlining the event, and I couldn't wait to see them perform.

I found a girl to hang with for the day. We popped some Adderall, drank some cocktails, and spent the day together. We were flying high, especially during Sevendust's set. After the show was over, I remember sitting in the bleachers with a bottle of vodka looking at the empty trash-filled stadium, thinking, "I've finally made it." What had I made? I was empty and lonely.

*War of Angels* was finally released with "Last Man Standing" as our first single. The song flew up the charts peaking out at number five. We now had a Top 5 single under our belt. This meant more radio play, and for me that meant larger royalty checks. We were already an active rock band, but "Last Man Standing" had a metal edge that would take us to another level. In the meantime, I was fighting to get sober. As much as I loved being drunk and high, it was beginning to take its toll on me. I tried to get clean, but it was always short-lived, especially on the road. That's where the party was.

We hit the road with Drowning Pool, and that didn't help my cause any. I was getting ripped every night on that tour. Every night I was slamming Jager Bombs. I'd satisfy myself with blow when it was available. We ended up getting a new tech for the road because our previous tech would get more trashed than us. We were the rock stars. If we were paying for a job to get done, we expected that job to get done and properly. The tour life continued on, and every night was like a rock and roll dream. I crossed paths with Billy Corgan (Smashing Pumpkins), Rob Zombie, Gene Simmons (Kiss), Riki Rachtman (host of MTV's Headbangers Ball), and many more.

On the Drowning Pool tour, my tech and I were having a conversation one night. It was just the two of us awake in the front lounge of the bus. Everyone else had gone to bed. He and I were hanging out, passing a bottle of Jack back and forth, talking about music and tattoos. We were en route to play a club called Pierre's in Ft. Wayne, Indiana. As we were discussing tattoos, we started talking about knuckle tattoos. I really wanted to get something tattooed across my knuckles. At the same time, I knew it had to be unique. I didn't want something generic and tacky. My tech said to me, "If I were to get knuckle tats, I'd get, F*** Y'all tattooed across my knuckles!" For whatever reason, in the moment, this seemed like the most brilliant thing I had ever heard of. I asked him if he was going to get it done. "No way," he responded, "My mom would kill me." Since he wasn't going to be using this "brilliant idea," I asked him if I could do it. I didn't want to steal it from him. "Sure," he said, "Go ahead!"

Not only was I going to do it, but I wasn't going to waste any time waiting. In just a few hours, we would be arriving at Pierre's, and I knew that there was a tattoo shop right next door that did pretty decent work. I planned on going right to the tattoo shop and getting this done as soon as we got there. Of course, I wasn't sober when I made this decision, but I was never sober! Sober was something that had gone out the window a long time ago. I told no one about the tattoo journey that I was about to embark on. I didn't want anyone trying to talk me out of it.

Several hours later, the moment we parked the bus, I got off and headed across the parking lot to the tattoo parlor. I hadn't been to bed yet. I had stayed up drinking all night. When I walked in and told the artist what I wanted done, he just looked at me and said, "Yeah, I can't do that." Even a tattoo artist had enough common sense to hesitate with something that crazy. He asked me, "How are you ever going to get a job?" I said, "I've got a job. I'm a rock star. I'm playing Pierre's next door." "Oh," he said. "In that case," he continued, "if you really want it done, I'll do it for you." We proceeded.

I walked out of that place like a proud peacock. I couldn't wait to show my band members what I had done. Some of them were shocked that I did it; some said nothing, and one called me his hero. I figured if we were going to be rebellious, we might as well go all in. I would play that night, putting my knuckles together towards the audience. The knuckle tats went great with other obscene artwork previously added to deface my body. Of course, for me, it was not defacing at all. It was the ultimate in freedom of expression. *War of Angels* was a hit album. After "Last Man Standing" peaked out at #5 on the billboards, we decided to release our second single, "Monster You Made", off of the album and got ready to shoot a video for it. We shot the video in Chicago, Illinois, close to where we were recording our album.

As the band got bigger, so did the shows, and so did the parties! Life became about the parties. Even if I had wanted to, I couldn't escape it. One night we played a festival in Dallas, headlined by Alice in Chains (who sounded amazing, by the way). Jerry Cantrell has an amazing tone. They tore it up that night. Since we were in Dallas, we were invited to go to The Clubhouse afterward. The Clubhouse was one of the "finest" strip clubs in all of Dallas, and it was owned by none other than Vinnie Paul from Pantera. There were naked women everywhere, and the place was flooded with rock stars. It seemed like Vinnie had invited every band from the festival to come out that night. I found myself at the bar, big surprise.

I had to get some drinks in me, not that I had stopped drinking. While waiting to get a drink at the bar, I noticed that Jerry Cantrell was standing right next to me. An older gentleman was standing next to Jerry, whom I assumed was his father. He had a work jacket on, and the place for his name said, "Rooster." I thought, "Can't be.

Could this really be the Rooster, the one who the song was about?" I introduced myself and asked him if that was him, and sure enough, it was. People were drunk and falling all over the place that night. Some guys literally couldn't balance themselves on their barstools.

The road was crazy, but being at home wasn't any better. I had no safe zone. On the road, I had to deal with myself, but at home, I had to deal with demons. The idea of demons in my life was not some metaphor but an absolute reality. Every once in awhile, we'd get a break and get to go home for a few days, sometimes up to a week or even a little longer. My home was a war zone. It was a hub for the supernatural. I would be lying in bed at night in the pitch-black darkness and yet manage to see black shadows racing across my room. Many strange and sudden events would occur at night. On one occasion, I heard two demons speaking to each other outside of my bedroom door. This was not something I heard in the spirit. I heard them audibly speaking to one another. They were speaking in some kind of an ancient language that I did not understand; to me, it sounded like Aramaic or Hebrew, but it wasn't either one of those. As the two demons spoke to each other, I knew they were talking about me. I also noticed that each one had a set of dual vocal cords. As it spoke, it had a super deep voice, with a second set of high vocal cords that sounded extremely feminine, speaking at the same exact time. As they spoke to each other, I sat and perked up in bed to listen, and they noticed. One said something to the other, possibly, "He can hear us," and they became completely silent.

There is no doubt that I wasn't alone. We are not alone. They are among us. There were times I would wake up out of a dead sleep at three o'clock in the morning to a pounding on the hallway wall right outside of my bedroom. It was being hit so hard that it seemed to shake the entire foundation of the house. The banging was violently loud. I would wake up to it in a state of panic, wondering what was going on, knowing all the while exactly what was going on.

One night before going back on the road, I heard tapping on the bedroom wall right next to my head. It tapped a particular rhythm over and over again for what seemed like hours. The next morning, I got picked up by the bus for our tour when I noticed that the tapping continued as I lay on my bunk. It was as if this thing was wherever I was. I didn't know how to escape the demons that were tormenting me; they were ever-present. I remember having a dream that stuck with me. In the dream, I was standing in a field, and there were other people standing in the field as well. It was a large open field surrounded by woods. Though it was nighttime and dark, everything seemed to be covered with a red tint.

In the dream, we were all looking up as if we had spotted something in the sky and lost it. We were all pointing and trying to figure what we had seen, but the sky was covered with a thick impenetrable haze. Suddenly, contraptions with lights began coming down through the fog and dropping these strange beings off. They looked like the predator, dreadlocks and all. They landed on one knee, then got up and came after the people. Someone in the dream shouted, "Run!" and everyone began running towards a house that was behind us in the dream, but these monsters were picking people off as they ran and devouring them. They were literally biting into and tearing people apart.

Very few people made it to the house, one of whom was me. As soon as we got in, I gave a command, "Board up the doors and the windows, because it won't be long before they come for us." The few of us who were in there quickly got the windows and doors boarded up, and we quietly waited. These creatures were demons who were out to steal, kill, and destroy as Jesus spoke about in the Gideon Bible I had snatched from the hotel: "The thief comes only to steal and kill and destroy." But I had yet to experience the promise of this verse where Jesus said of Himself, "I have come that they may have life, and that they may have it more abundantly," (John 10:10 NKJV). Soon, I would.

Though we were having amazing success as a band, I was in the worst place of my life, spiritually, mentally, and physically. I was exhausted. To be quite frank, I didn't want to live anymore. I was depressed and becoming more and more suicidal by the day. At times I would just flip out and start attacking myself. I'd punch myself in the face. I hated being me. It got to a point where I was on a suicide watch, although nobody said anything to me about it. On the outside, it looked like I had my life together, but on the inside I was dying. I couldn't shake these devils, and I certainly couldn't get away from myself. I had become my own worst enemy. No matter what, I couldn't win. It was as if I were drowning, and there was no rescue boat coming, none that I could see anyway. I was trapped. I was caught up in a lifestyle that I could not escape. The pills, drinking, and drugs had consumed me, and so did my appetite for women and sex. It seemed like no matter how much I indulged myself, it was never enough. I desperately needed help. I needed an answer.

# MY PORCELAIN ALTAR

We were five years deep into touring, and I was now on the biggest tour of my life. We were out on the road again with Theory of a Deadman and Three Doors Down, playing stadiums every single night. I loved playing stadium shows. From that moment when I had seen White Zombie in that stadium as a little boy, I set out to accomplish just that. Here I was, all these years later, fulfilling my dream, yet there was no fulfillment in it. Nonetheless the tour itself was amazing. Each night we'd meet backstage to do a band huddle before taking the stage. The band was going nowhere but up.

One night after a show, I asked my tour manager if I could have the night off. The band was going to some VIP event, but I knew that I needed to stay back and rest. He agreed with me. He said, "I'll tell you what, we're all going out, and we're going to come back and crash on the bus tonight. Why don't you take the hotel room by yourself, and get all the rest that you want." He handed me the key to the room, and I made my way to it. I was just burned out. Between the shows, the partying, and the girls, a body can only take so much.

I went up to the hotel room and ran a hot bath. I just wanted to sit in the tub and relax.

As I sat in that bathtub, I was met with complete silence. Silence on the road is rare, especially when you live on a bus with nine guys. But suddenly, my life was eerily quiet. It was almost too quiet. It felt as if there was a second man in the room with me. As I sat there in that bathtub, I began to reflect on my life. With all of the success I'd had up to this point, how could I be so miserable? It was in that moment that God spoke to me and said, "I created you for a relationship with Me, and it'll never work without Me." Why would God want a relationship with me? Why would he want to hang out with some drunk? I didn't understand; nevertheless, I longed for that relationship.

As I pondered the words spoken deep within my spirit, conviction set in, and I said, "God, you know everything that I've done, but You need to hear it from my mouth. I'm sick and tired of hiding from You, and I'm sick and tired of running." As I began to confess my sins to the Lord, I broke down and began to weep in that bathtub. Suddenly, it became my porcelain altar. "I'm so sorry Lord," I sobbed, "Please forgive me, I didn't know what I was doing."

At that moment, I sensed the Lord speaking to me, "Son, I forgive you; now I'm going to give you the One who's going to empower you." Before I could even respond to that statement, the Holy Spirit came, and the power of God hit me and began to surge through me. It was as if invisible jumper cables had been hooked up to my body sending an immense amount of power into me. It was surging. I stopped crying, and that power sat me up and turned me to the right. My eyes locked on the previously unnoticed tissue box under the sink. The word written across that box was *Heavenly.* God wanted me to know that I was forgiven. The moment my eyes connected with that box, the power ceased from entering me.

I quickly realized that something else miraculous had happened in those moments. Not only was I forgiven and now a born again child of God, but all of my addictions were gone. The Lord took them. I felt so free and clean. It was as if they never existed at all. I got out of the tub at that moment and went straight to bed.

In one night, in a single moment, everything in my life changed. The next morning when I walked out of my hotel room to head down to the bus, I was keenly aware that the pain, addictions, and hate that had previously filled me were gone. My life was now filled with a peace and a love that I had never felt before. I was no longer my own, but I was His child. I was a born-again Christian. The God Who died for me came to me and saved me. When I walked onto the tour bus, I felt like an alien in my own environment. What once felt like home and safety suddenly had become a place of danger and insecurity, though I felt secure in the fact that God was with me. I walked back to my bunk, not sure what to say to anyone. I climbed into my bunk and closed the curtain. I lay there knowing that everything had changed and that my life would never be the same again.

"What just happened?" I pondered. As free as I was, the war was just beginning. I began to face ridicule and persecution for my new-found faith. All I knew was that I wanted to share this joy that I now possessed with the world; not only did I *want* to share it with the rest of the world, but I knew that it was my *obligation* to do so. No one in my life could understand the sudden and radical transformation that had taken place in me. The Apostle Paul wrote, "Therefore, if anyone is in Christ, the new creation has come: The old is gone, the new is here!" (2 Corinthians 5:17, NIV).

Everything had been made new and had shifted. People in my life only knew me as a drunk, rock and roll womanizing rebel, but that old man was gone, and Anthony Greve had emerged. Radio stations around the country were beginning to talk about how I was losing my mind because all I wanted to talk about was Christ. Matter of fact, I began to use my Facebook platform to share with people the Hope of the World, that Hope being Jesus Christ. For the next several months, I continued to tour with the band, knowing that it would only be a matter of time before I exited.

I couldn't get enough of the Word of God. A life that once consisted of regular alcohol consumption and drugs was now filled with daily prayer and the Bible. If we weren't playing a show, my nose was buried deep in the Word. I no longer spent my after-hours partying with fans, but I began to seize opportunities to pray for and minister to people. I called someone I knew who was a brother in Christ to share my new found faith with him. "It's like I have new eyes and new ears," I said. He replied, "You're talking the Bible, and you don't even know it."

I called a band meeting. We were still out on the road with Theory of a Deadman and Three Doors Down. The band had no idea what the meeting was about, and I could tell that people were nervous about it because in my entire history with the band, I had never called a band meeting for any reason. When the tour manager gathered everyone together, they learned that the meeting was to announce my new faith to the band. I thanked everyone for their time and said, "I called this meeting together, because I want you guys to know that I gave my life to Jesus Christ and accepted Him as my Lord and Savior. I don't entirely know what all this means yet, but I want you to know where I stand."

It was necessary to verbalize my position even though everyone was aware of where I stood. It was important to take a stand because I no longer fit into this world that I once belonged to. Instead, I had been born into a new Kingdom. How could I explain it to anyone? I wasn't even sure that it was explainable. God was calling me to be a leader in His Kingdom. This was a call to ministry and specifically to evangelism. All I wanted to do was win souls for Jesus. Looking out the window of the bus one day as we were traveling I thought, "I could do what I'm doing now but for Jesus. I can travel around and win people for Christ."

The next stop on our tour was Ft. Wayne, Indiana. We parked in a Walmart parking lot for the night. We did this from time to time because Walmart was generally open twenty-four/seven, which gave us something to do. We could shop and use the restrooms if need be. Next to Walmart was a Family Christian store. I was longing for someone to pray with. I decided to go into the store and check it out. As I did, I wondered if the employees even believed in Jesus or if this was just a job for them. I went to the back of the store and was browsing the books. An employee had just come out of the back and was carrying a stack of boxes. "Can I help you with anything?" he asked, and I replied with my own question, "Do you believe in Jesus?"

"Oh, I sure do!" the employee responded. I asked him if he would be willing to pray with me. At that moment, a youth pastor who was also an evangelist just happened to walk by. The store employee, who obviously knew the man, grabbed him and asked if he would pray with us. I stood there praying with these complete strangers (though known in the Spirit), and tears began to run down my cheeks. I was overwhelmed with the presence and love of God.

As I left the store, I'll never forget what that evangelist said to me: "You're at the crossroads of your life, dawg, choose the cross." I knew I was facing a difficult choice ahead. I knew I couldn't stay in the environment I was in, not if I wanted to survive.

The tour went on. Even in the midst of the tour life, I was experiencing the miraculous hand of God. There was a girl who interviewed us who had a disease with her vocal cords and could talk no higher than a whisper. She was told that she'd never regain normal use of her vocal cords again. I reached out to her and asked her if she believed in God. She did. I asked if she believed that God could heal her. She did. I prayed for her. A few days later, she called me, speaking in a completely normal voice, to let me know that God had touched her and completely healed her vocal cords. The disease was gone. It was a complete miracle.

Aside from the wonderful exhilaration of witnessing the miraculous, I was feeling pressure from both sides of the fence. I knew that God was calling me to leave that world, but there was a fight from those who wanted me to stay in it. How was I going to go into ministry? How was I going to save all of these lost people? What would the implications be if I walked away? I had no support from the outside, and I felt like I was completely alone in this. People thought I had gone crazy, and because of the backlash I was receiving, I even started to question myself.

Succumbing to the pressure, I ended up staying in the band. It felt like there was no way out. I felt completely trapped. I believed that I was strong enough to stay in it and walk out my walk, but it would only be a matter of time before I'd fall back into my old habits and way of living. That's exactly what happened. Little by little, I drifted back into the rock and roll lifestyle of drinking, popping pills, and partying; the only difference was I was more miserable than ever before. I had believed that God was going to get me out of it, and now here I was, completely stuck.

When the tour ended, we had a few weeks off to relax and regroup. I wanted to take this time to get my mind straight. Things seem to have escalated. I was becoming aware of the increasing activity of the supernatural and the spiritual warfare that was taking place in my home. I remember standing in the kitchen and seeing flashing lights throughout the house. In the natural, I thought that maybe something was going on with my eyes. But this wasn't internal; this was something external taking place around me. The flashes of lights looked like bulb flashes from an old-time camera. It was as if the paparazzi were behind me taking pictures. The flashing lights became frequent. It was during this period that God began to speak to me about reading my Bible again.

Because of my backslidden state, I felt convicted and didn't want to read my Bible, but for the next three days, as the flashing lights continued around me, God continued to speak to me about reading my Bible. He told me to read one Scripture verse, Mark 9:26. With September 26th being my birthday, this stood out to me. God wasn't letting up, so I decided to read the verse. I got out my Bible and opened it to Mark 9:26. It read: "The spirit shrieked, convulsed him violently and came out. The boy looked so much like a corpse that many said, 'He's dead' (NIV)."

I didn't understand what God was trying to say to me by giving me this verse. I thought that maybe it meant that I was demon possessed. I called a local church for answers. Though this particular church was helpful and let me know they didn't think I was demon possessed, they did think I was oppressed. Being possessed means you have a demon (or demons) in you; being oppressed means, there is a demon (or demons) harassing you.

Although the church gave me good advice, they didn't want to move forward until I had seen a doctor and ruled out any possibility that what I was facing was medical. This frustrated me. I knew that this would give the enemy leverage because I knew what I was facing was spiritual and not physical. In my frustration, I didn't know what to do. The following day I ran into an old friend at the gas station. When he asked me how I was doing, I proceeded to fill him in on the craziness that had been taking place in my life. "My sister has dealt with spirits before, and she may be able to help you out," he said. I just needed answers. He gave me his sister's number, and I called her. She agreed to come and assess my situation. She was a medium who worked in the realm of dealing with spirits. At this point, I was willing to try anything as I was still searching for answers. I knew that God was the solution, but I did not know how to deal with what was taking place in my home.

The next evening she came to the house. She seemed pleasant and non-threatening. She had brought a Ouija board with her and asked if she could bring it in. I allowed her to. When she walked into my room, she was instantly overwhelmed by the presence of darkness. "Whoa!" she exclaimed, "I have never felt anything like this before.". From the hallway into my bedroom, the atmosphere drastically seemed to shift. It was like walking into a heavy blanket of oppression. She lit a candle, and we shut off the lights. The moment we did, the wind chimes outside of my bedroom window began to rattle against each other creating an eerie sound and feeling that permeated the room. The strange thing was, it had been a completely still night up until this point. There was no wind.

When we spoke to the board, I first asked if whoever was present had made those wind chimes go off. With a strong pull, the plastic piece mediating strongly pulled to the word, "Yes." The pull was strong. It was evident that there was a third party involved. I asked if I was speaking to someone who had died in the house. It responded, "No." I asked if I was speaking to my grandfather, who had passed away in Turkey. The plastic piece on the board pulled strongly towards the word, "Yes." Could it be? Could the spirit that I was communicating with now be that of my deceased grandfather? How could I be sure?

I asked, "If you really are my grandfather, what kind of music did you ask me to play on the guitar for you when I was a kid?" It responded, "C O W B O Y," moving to one letter at a time. To play cowboy music was my grandfather's way of saying country music. To get confirmation that it was him, I asked another personal question, "What was your favorite type of drink to drink?" It spelled out, "R A K…" "Do you mean Raki?" I asked, which was a Turkish liquor. It responded by quickly moving to the word yes. Though it was answering my questions, I wasn't convinced that it was him. Something felt off and not right about the whole thing. The woman left and decided to leave the Ouija board with me in case I wanted to use it anymore.

That night my friend Landon was coming over to the house for pizza and movies. Landon arrived about ten minutes after the medium left. He could sense the strangeness in the house. While we were waiting for the oven to heat up for the pizza, I looked up and noticed a white, smoke-like cloud was accumulating at the ceiling, and it was flowing down the hallway and going into my bedroom. It seemed odd that the smoke was only turning off into my bedroom. I decided to walk down to my bedroom and have a look.

The smoke was disappearing once it hit the atmosphere of my room. This was so strange. I was trying to figure out what was going on. I followed the stream of smoke from my bedroom back to the kitchen. I noticed the smoke, like steam, rising from the back of the stove. At first, it looked like it was coming from the tea kettle on the stove, but the more I examined it, I realized it was coming from the back of the stove. "Why is this smoking?" I thought. That's when I realized that the oven was on fire. Landon and I began to splash water into the oven until we finally got the fire put out. You could feel the intensity in the air. "What's going on here?" Landon said. The moment he said that the computer hard drive went haywire and sounded like it was about to take off. It kicked into overdrive and was like a running motor. I got it unplugged, and it shut off. I looked at Landon and said, "Why don't we call it a night?"

# THE OUIJA BOARD

The strange occurrences continued. The next day I noticed my cat very cautiously walking around the Ouija board box and sniffing it. I went to check it out and noticed that ice-cold air was blowing out of the creases of the box. Everything seemed strange. I had been dating a girl from Indiana at that time. Her name was Miranda. She was coming to visit and stay with me for the weekend. Miranda was a beautiful girl with jet black hair. We had been dating on and off since my decision not to depart from the band. When she came over, I said, "Hey, we gotta check out this Ouija board, this thing is for real." Miranda used it with me. We lit a candle and went through the whole procedure. This time, the entity speaking to us proceeded to tell us that its name was Aaron and that it had come through a portal in Heaven.

After several minutes of speaking to us, "Aaron" moved the plastic piece to "Goodbye" on the board, and it stopped. I turned the lights on, and said to Miranda, "Isn't it interesting? Our lives are a lot like that candle. We both need oxygen to survive, and when it's over, poof!" The moment I said, "Poof," the candle went out and a bright orange flame shot up like a torch. It went out and shot up like a torch three times. The third time, it slowly went out, filling the room with a cloud of black smoke. As odd as this all was, Miranda didn't overthink it. However, as she and I were sitting on my bed having a conversation, I noticed that her eyes were turning bloodshot red and that she was twitching.

"Stop it," I said. "Stop what?" she asked. I said, "You're twitching." "No, I'm not," she said. "Yes, you are," I responded. Then suddenly, she would start twitching again, then she tipped her head back and breathed out a long drawn-in breath, and I could see her breath as if she were in an icebox or outside on a cold winter day, only it was somewhere around seventy-six degrees in the house. Miranda left at the end of that weekend, and we stopped dating soon after that.

The supernatural activity that was taking place was through the roof. I called Landon and invited him over along with another one of our friends, Gabe. I needed witnesses to what was going on. I wasn't crazy. I said to Landon and Gabe, "Listen, you guys, there has been crazy stuff going on in this house. I need to show you guys what's been happening." Even though they didn't fully believe me, about the board, they complied and agreed to give me a chance to prove it. We sat at my kitchen table for about a half an hour with the Ouija board, and nothing worked. Finally, I said to them, "Guys, let's try one more thing. If nothing happens, we can chalk it up to me being crazy and call it a night." We then moved from the kitchen to my bedroom to see if we could get a response from the board. Landon and I were in front of the Ouija board at the end of the bed while Gabe was sitting on the other end of the bed watching us. The plastic point of contact began to move. Suddenly, the atmosphere shifted, and it felt like something was about to go terribly wrong. Landon screamed out in pain as a demon entered his body. As it entered him, his face went completely blank, his arms contorted and stiffened by his sides as this demon slowly lifted him up off his knees and threw him onto his back across the room. Frightened, I jumped back, pressing up against the wall as Gabe sat on the end of the bed speechless and stunned.

Landon's facial features had changed as if he had taken on the look of the demon that possessed him. The hatred and evil emanating from him were unlike anything I had ever felt or experienced before. It wasn't human. The demon in Landon began to huff and puff as if it were about to speak. In that moment, I heard the Lord say, "Mark 9:26. Cast out that devil, boy." Power and boldness began to fill the room. At that moment I lunged forward, palming Landon's head and shouting, "With all the power of God in Heaven, and in the name of Jesus Christ of Nazareth, I command you to come out of his body!"

As I took authority over the demon, Landon's body began to violently convulse at the name of Jesus, and his eyes were completely rolled back in his head. You could only see the whites of his eyes through his fluttering eyelids. Finally, the shaking ceased, and the demon was gone. Landon woke up groggy as if from a deep sleep, having no recollection of what had just taken place.

My faith was reignited in the face of this evidence that what Jesus had said was true: We would cast out devils in His name (Mark 16:17). Since that truth was just confirmed in my presence, for me, it also confirmed that the rest of the Bible was true.

At the end of our break, the band had a one-off show that we were playing in Battle Creek, Michigan. After the Battle Creek show, we had another two weeks off, and then we were hitting the road with Theory of a Deadman. With all of these recent events taking place, I had already made up my mind that I was leaving the band.

I was leaving the music industry, and that I was walking away from any lifestyle which glorified sin. I showed up to the Battle Creek show on fire for God. Though I knew my time in the band would be short, I was excited to be taking the stage that night. I had already made up my mind that I was going to rock this show for Jesus. When we took the stage, I noticed a fan of ours who was there front and center. He was usually always at our Michigan shows, only this time when I looked at him, chills shot through my entire body. What was in Landon the night before was now here in this Pop Evil fan.

I didn't move. The band began to rock out, but it suddenly felt like I was in a different arena, like I wasn't even there. Normally fans would engage with me and I with them, but it was like no one even noticed me. Every once in awhile, I would look up at this fan, only to see this evil look of hatred towards me. I ran over side stage and said to our tour manager, Jed, "Make sure these access points are guarded." I didn't want that "fan" getting back there. I watched as the demon in this individual made movements towards certain individuals as if he was controlling them like puppets on strings. He seemed to be in control over the entire crowd, which is interesting since the Bible regards Satan as, "The prince of the air" (Ephesians 2:2).

I watched as the demon in this man turned and looked at individuals like he wanted to devour them. At one point, I shrugged my shoulders towards him as if to say, "What's the deal?" He shouted, "I'm really ticked off!" I knew I was in a fight with the devil. Suddenly, the Spirit of God spoke to me and said, "Son, you have one foot in the world and one foot in my Kingdom, you have to make a choice." It was at that moment I decided I was leaving Pop Evil *immediately*. After the show, I decided to get out of town. I had to getaway. I drove home, packed a suitcase, and grabbed a couple of my guitars. I would be hitting the road again, only this time not for a tour. I left the state of Michigan. I decided to lay low with some friends of mine in Ohio. It was the only safe place that I knew for the time being.

When I arrived in Ohio, I shot the band an email, letting them know that my decision was final and that I was leaving the band and the music industry. It was time to walk in the calling that God had placed on my life. That week I walked into a church while a worship team was rehearsing, and I got down on my knees at the altar and said, "God, now I give You my life. I give You my band, my career, and all that I am. I surrender it all to You. Use me to fulfill Your purposes on this earth." Though it was the end of a chapter, it was just the beginning of my journey with God.

# OUTRO

*A message to you, the reader*

L eaving Pop Evil and walking away from the music industry didn't come without trials, battles, and tribulations. It cost me many relationships (some of which God has since restored). He has also brought into my life relationships that I would have never had otherwise. There is a cost to picking up your cross and following Jesus. It's a cost that most aren't willing to pay. However, on the other side of that cross is the fulfillment, satisfaction, and journey that we are all looking for.

The reward of overcoming one battle is that you get to fight your next battle. Following my departure from the music world, the next several months of my journey with God took me around the country. It was in this time that I allowed God to grow me, direct me, and minister to me. These were difficult times of growth, and yet they contained beautiful times of transformation. It was in these moments and places that I learned valuable lessons. God taught me the importance of the supernatural and how deeply involved He is in every area of our lives. My journey led me from Michigan, Ohio, West Virginia, and to other states, eventually leading me back to

Michigan. When you step out to walk on the water with God, and to take a journey with Him, there is going to have to be much trust involved. When you step out into the realm of the unknown, you are trusting the God you know to meet you there. God is and has been faithful every step of the way. He met me, cared for me, and provided for my needs. These were special moments in my life that I will never forget.

Having stepped out of the music industry to answer the call of God on my life, I was led to Northpoint Bible College in Haverhill, Massachusetts in 2013, where I would spend the next four years of my life learning and studying the Word of God, while developing and learning how to trust and depend on God. God was grooming and preparing me for full-time ministry. In 2016, God led me to begin my evangelistic ministry, Anthony Greve Ministries. Since then we have been plowing ground, ministering, and teacher others the Word of God. I graduated from Northpoint Bible College in 2017 with a Bachelor of Arts degree. I majored in Biblical Theology while minoring in Pastoral Studies.

You will never outgrow your dependency on God because you were created for it. Though the seasons change, God remains the same, and so does our need for Him. Today, pushing forward in full-time ministry, I've learned how to depend on God more than ever. He is, and will forever be, my Source.

The Bible tells us in John 3:3 that unless a man is born again, he cannot enter the Kingdom of God. Romans 3:23 says, "For all have sinned and fall short of the glory of God" (NIV). You see, according to the Word of God, we have all sinned and fallen short of His glory. Ever since sin entered the world through the disobedience of Adam and Eve, "When the woman saw that the fruit of the tree was good for food and pleasing to the eye, and also desirable for gaining wisdom, she took some and ate it. She also gave some to her husband, who was with her, and he ate it. Then the eyes of both of them were opened, and they realized they were naked; so they sewed fig leaves together and made coverings for themselves." (Genesis 3:6-7, NIV), man has been suffering at the hand of the enemy as a consequence of his actions.

The fall brought poverty, sickness, disease, tragedy, and death into our world. We were cursed. The Bible tells us that sin separated us from God "But your iniquities have separated you from your God; And your sins have hidden His face from you, So that He will not hear." (Isaiah 59:2, NKJV). Sin cannot enter into the presence of God. The only way for man to be made right with God was for God to send His only Son into the world to pay the price for our sins and save us, "For God so loved the world that He gave His only begotten Son, that whoever believes in Him should not perish but have everlasting life." (John 3:16, NKJV).

Right now, you may be saying, "I've done too much wrong, I've made too many mistakes, and there is no way that God could ever forgive me." You read my store; If God could forgive me, He can and will forgive you! You might say that He put this book into your hands so that you would know how willing He is to forgive you. He wants you to know how much He loves you.

In the beginning of this book, I mentioned how important it is not to lose the ability to dream. There is an enemy of your soul who has tried to steal your dreams, perhaps dreams you had as a child that have almost been forgotten. Not only does he want to steal your dreams, but your life. In the Gospel of John (10:10) in the New Testament it says, "A thief has only one thing in mind – he wants to steal, slaughter (kill), and destroy. But I have come to give you everything in abundance, more than you expect – life in its fullness until you overflow!" (TPT). No one should ever let the devil steal his or her dreams. I pray that every dream of yours that was stolen will be restored ten-fold by God. He has amazing things in store for you (read Jeremiah 29:11). He has amazing plans for your life!

God paid the ultimate price for you and me to be saved. He gave His very life, in the Person of His Son, on a cross a little over two thousand years ago in Jerusalem so that you and I could be made right with Him. The Bible tells us that all we have to do to receive this salvation is believe and confess that Jesus Christ is Lord. Romans 10:9 says, "If you declare with your mouth, 'Jesus is Lord,' and believe in your heart that God raised Him from the dead, you will be saved" (NIV). Salvation is a free gift, and all you have to do is believe that Jesus died to give you new life in order to receive it. That's why I have included the salvation prayer on the next page for you to pray so that you can receive Jesus Christ as your Lord and Savior and enter into eternal life today. Pray it out loud right now if you want to give your life to Jesus. Today is your day! Don't wait another moment to be saved.

# SALVATION PRAYER

**Instructions: In order to accept Jesus Christ into your heart, say this prayer out loud!**

*Lord Jesus, I ask You to come into my heart today and to forgive me of all of my sins. I repent, I turn from my sin, and I ask for Your cleansing blood and grace to transform my life. Wash me, cleanse me, and give me a new start. I believe that You died for my sins and rose again on the third day, and today I invite You to be my Lord and my Savior. According to my own confession, I am saved, I am cleansed, I've been made right with You, and Heaven is my home. In Jesus' Name, Amen.*

### *Congratulations on getting saved!*

*If you made that decision to get saved today, your next steps are to start reading the Bible, develop a prayer life, and get connected and plugged into a good Bible believing church. I pray that this story has tremendously blessed, helped, and benefited you in multiple ways. If you prayed that prayer for the first time or prayed it in a re-dedication of your life to Jesus, I would love to hear about it and connect with you. Please visit my website to learn more and to contact me:*

### *www.anthonygreveministries.com*

*Sincerely and in His service,*
*Anthony Greve*

CPSIA information can be obtained
at www.ICGtesting.com
Printed in the USA
LVHW071641300621
691545LV00022B/2039